The

Abingdon Worship
Annual 2020

WORSHIP PLANNING
RESOURCES FOR
EVERY SUNDAY OF THE YEAR

The

Abingdon Worship
Annual 2020

(800) 247-4784

Edited by
Mary Scifres
and B.J. Beu

Abingdon Press / Nashville

The Abingdon Worship Annual 2020

WORSHIP PLANNING RESOURCES
FOR VERY SUNDAY OF THE YEAR

Copyright © 2019 by Abingdon Press

This book is printed on acid-free paper.

ISBN 978-1-5018-8170-1

19 20 21 22 23 24 25 26 27 28—10 9 8 7 6 5 4 3 2 1

MANUFACTURED IN THE UNITED STATES OF AMERICA

Contents

September

October

November

CONTENTS

December

Introduction

For many people, worship is the only activity that leads them into an awareness of God's presence in their lives. As such, worship planning becomes a sacred undertaking, which is both joyous and sobering. Though we would love to have uninterrupted time each week to devote to worship planning, our schedules often leave us little choice but to fit it in among the myriad tasks and responsibilities placing demands on our time. This problem becomes even more pronounced when worship leaders are faced with demands for diverse music and worship styles, and eye-catching on-screen presentations. Add in multimedia, visuals, texting, tweeting, and visitors "liking" your church on Facebook (during worship), and the pressures placed upon worship planners can become overwhelming.

For these reasons, *The Abingdon Worship Annual 2020* is invaluable as a resource and partner in your planning process. In this resource, we provide theme ideas and all the written and spoken elements of worship, following the Revised Common Lectionary. (Although the *Worship Annual* does not address the visual and emerging resources that many worship services require, Mary's *Worship Resource Subscription* provides all of these materials, available at **www.maryscifresministries.com/worship-resources**.) *The Abingdon Worship Annual 2020* offers words for worship that provide the framework for congregations to participate fully in the liturgical life of worship.

In *The Abingdon Worship Annual 2020*, you will find the words of many different authors, poets, pastors, laypersons, and theologians. Some authors have written for this resource before, others provide a fresh voice. Since the contributing authors represent a wide variety of denominational and theological backgrounds, their words will vary in style and content. Feel free to combine or adjust the words within these pages to fit the needs of your congregation and the style of your worship. (Notice the reprint permission for worship given on the copyright page of this book.)

Each entry provides suggestions that follow an order of service that may be adapted to address your specific worship practice and format. Feel free to reorder or pick and choose the various resources to fit the needs of your worship services and congregations. Each entry follows a thematic focus arising from one or more of the week's scriptures.

To fit the Basic Pattern of Christian Worship—reflecting a flow that leads from a time of gathering and praise, into a time of receiving and responding to the Word, and ending with a time of sending forth—each entry includes Contemporary Gathering Words, Call to Worship, and Opening Prayer, Prayer of Confession and Words of Assurance, Response to the Word, Offertory Prayer, and Benedictions. Communion resources are offered in selected entries. Additional ideas are also provided throughout this resource.

Some readers find the Contemporary Gathering Words or Unison Prayers helpful as "Centering Words" that may be printed in a worship handout or projected on a screen. Use the words offered here in the way the best suits your congregation's spiritual needs, and please remember to give copyright and author credit!

Using the Worship Resources

Contemporary Gathering Words and **Calls to Worship** gather God's people together as they prepare to worship. Often called "Greetings" or "Gathering Words," these words may be read by one worship leader or responsively. Regardless of how they are printed in this resource, feel free to experiment in your services of worship. They may be read antiphonally (back and forth) between two readers or two groups within the congregation: women and men, choir and musicians, young people and old, etc.

Opening Prayers in this resource are varied in form, but typically invoke God's presence into worship. Whether formal, informal, general, or specific, these prayers serve to attune our hearts and minds to God. Although many may be adapted for use in other parts of the worship service, we have grouped them into the category "Opening Prayers."

Prayers of Confession and **Words of Assurance** lead the people of God to acknowledge our failing while assuring us of God's forgiveness and grace. Regardless of how they are printed, whether unison or responsively, Prayers of Confession and Words of Assurance may be spoken by a single leader or led by a small group. Some prayers may even be used as Opening or Closing Prayers.

Litanies and **Responsive Readings** offer additional avenues of congregational participation in our services of worship. Think creatively as you decide how to use these **Responsive Readings** in your service of worship: in unison, by a worship leader alone, or in a call-and-response format. Feel free to change the title of these liturgies to suit your worship setting.

Benedictions, sometimes called "Blessings" or "Words of Dismissal," send the congregation forth to continue the work of worship in the world. Some of these Benedictions work best as a call-and-response; others work best when delivered as a blessing by a single worship leader. As always, use the format best suited to your congregation.

In response to requests from many of our readers, we have provided a number of **Communion** liturgies as well, each written specifically to relate to the thematic and scriptural focus of the day. Some follow the pattern of the Great Thanksgiving; others are Invitations to Communion or Communion Prayers of Consecration for the celebration of the Eucharist.

Although you will find *The Abingdon Worship Annual 2020* an invaluable tool for planning worship, it is but one piece of the puzzle for worship preparation. For additional music suggestions, you will want to consult *Prepare! An Ecumenical Music and Worship Planner*, or *The United Methodist Music and Worship Planner*. These resources contain lengthy listings of lectionary-related hymns, praise songs, vocal solos, and choral anthems. As a final complement to your worship planning process, Mary also pens *Worship Plans and Ideas* as part of her worship subscription service, including video and film-clip suggestions, screen visuals, popular song ideas, and hands-on participation suggestions, along with series ideas, suggested sermon titles, and sermon starters for each Sunday. Explore Mary's *Worship Resource Subscription* at **www.maryscifresministries .com/worship-resources.**

As you begin your worship planning, read the scriptures for each day, then meditate on the **Theme Ideas** suggested in this resource. Review the many words for worship printed herein and listen for the words that speak to you. Trust God's guidance, and enjoy a wonderful year of worship and praise!

Mary Scifres and B. J. Beu, Editors
The Abingdon Worship Annual
beuscifres@gmail.com

January 1, 2020

Watch Night/New Year
Linda Hess

Color

White

Scripture Readings

Ecclesiastes 3:1-13; Psalm 8;
Revelation 21:1-6a; Matthew 25:31-46

Theme Ideas

God is the giver of all that we experience. Whether we
view our experiences positively or negatively is largely
up to us and affects our approach to life. Looking to God
in all of life's circumstances is vital to experiencing the gift
of eternal life promised through Christ. Our interconnect-
edness with one another is essential to our connection to
God, and the way we respond to the needs of others is a
visible demonstration of our relationship with God.

Invitation and Gathering

Call to Worship (Ps 8, Eccl 3, Rev 21)
O Lord, our Lord, how majestic is your name
in all the earth!
You have set your glory above the heavens.

From the lips of children and infants,
you ordain praise and thanksgiving
to silence the foe and the avenger.
You make everything beautiful in its own time.
You set eternity in our hearts,
yet we cannot fathom what you have done
from beginning to end.
What could be better than to be happy
and to do good while we live?
O Lord, our Lord, how majestic is your name
in all the earth!
O God, our God, you are Alpha and Omega,
the beginning and the end.

—*Or*—

Call to Worship (Matt 25)

All who hunger and thirst are welcome here.
Come find the food and drink
that does not perish.
All who are strangers are welcome here.
When it's time to leave,
we'll part as friends.
All who don't know where to turn are welcome here.
Come and find the living God,
who helps us find our way.
Thanks be to God.

Opening Prayer (Rev 21, Matt 25)

We come to you today, God,
the Alpha and the Omega,
as people blessed by your tender care.
We come as people who are hungry,
thirsty, sick, imprisoned,
and strangers to one another.

Help us do as you ask,
>and meet each other's needs.
Today, we come to seek your guidance,
>that we may better understand how to follow
>>the teaching of Christ, our Lord and Savior,
>>>in whose name we pray. Amen.

Proclamation and Response

Prayer of Confession (Eccl 3)
Gracious God, giver of new beginnings,
we come to you today, confessing our need.
>**As we face this coming year,**
>**help us through each day.**
As we leave the past year behind,
help us look to you.
>**When we face birth or death;**
>**when we confront a time to plant or to uproot,**
>**help us put our faith in you.**
When we see a time to tear down or to build up;
When we face a time to weep or to laugh;
When we meet a time to be silent or a time to speak,
help us rely on you.
>**You alone know what the coming year holds.**
>**You alone know of our small triumphs**
>**and our grand failures.**
Gracious God, assure us once again
that there is forgiveness in your love.
>**Heal us with the knowledge**
>**that our sins may be left with you,**
>**through our savior, Jesus Christ. Amen.**

Words of Assurance (Eccl 3:1, 11a, Matt 25:34)
God brings a season for every activity under heaven
    and has made everything beautiful in its time.
Although we cannot fathom the depths of God's love,
    we know that God cares for each of us;
    we know that our inheritance comes from God.

Passing the Peace of Christ (Phil 4:7a NIV)
May the peace of God, which passes all understanding,
be with you. Share this gift of peace as you turn to great
one another.

Response to the Word (Matt 25, Ps 8, Eccl 3)
Let all who are blessed by God,
    come and take your inheritance.
In your hearts, receive the gift of eternal life
    promised by God.
Celebrate the majesty of God's name in all the earth!

—Or—

Response to the Word (Ps 8)
God, you are an awesome and a mighty God!
    We see your glory in the heavens above
    and in the earth below.
We see the work of your hands
when we behold the moon and the stars.
    We see you in everything that is.
We see the work of your fingers
when we look at the flocks and herds,
the beasts of the field, the birds of the air,
and the fish of the sea.
    We praise your name continually
    and marvel at your creation.

God, you are an awesome and a mighty God!
**We see your glory in the heavens above
and in the earth below.**

Thanksgiving and Communion

Invitation to the Offering (Matt 25 NIV)

We are here to give our gifts, as Jesus has taught us. To those who are hungry and thirsty, let us offer food and drink, that they may be satisfied. To those in need of clothing, let us offer raiment to clothe them. To those who are sick, let us offer them our care. To those in prison, let us offer the gift of our presence, as we visit them. We remember, as Jesus has told us, that whatever we do for the least of our brothers and sisters, we do for Christ. May the gifts we give today be a demonstration of our love for God, and may they maintain and expand the work of this congregation.

Offering Prayer (Matt 25)

God, source of all that we have,
    help us remember the tasks you have set before us.
Take these gifts today,
    that they may help continue
        the work we are called to do.
Use this place and this congregation
    to reflect the love that Christ has shown us.
In your holy name, we pray. Amen.

Sending Forth

Benediction (Eccl 3 NIV)
Go forth with happiness and with good works.
   This is what God has called us to do.
Find satisfaction in all your toil.
   This is the gift of God.
In everything you do, praise the Lord.
   Amen!

January 5, 2020

Epiphany of the Lord Sunday
B. J. Beu

Color

White

Scripture Readings

Isaiah 60:1-6; Psalm 72:1-7, 10-14; Ephesians 3:1-12; Matthew 2:1-12

Theme Ideas

Today's scripture readings are much more than a celebration of kings bringing tribute to the Messiah; they are *magi* a promise of light to those who live in darkness, a promise of righteousness to those who suffer at the hands of others, a promise of grace to those who are lost, and a promise of salvation to the Gentiles. Epiphany is a day to celebrate God's love for all—especially those who are most in need of God's light and love.

Invitation and Gathering

Centering Words (Isa 60, Matt 2)

Light shines in the darkness, and the darkness fades like a passing dream. Will we turn in reverence to the light, or will we turn away, distracted by other things? Follow the light of the world.

Call to Worship (Isa 60)

Arise, shine! Your light has come.
The glory of the Lord shines like the sun.
Behold, the nations have come to witness God's light.
Kings have come to behold Christ's brightness.
Lift up your eyes and look around.
The glory of the Lord is all around.
Arise, shine! Your light has come.

—Or—

Call to Worship (Ps 72)

The Holy One rules.
Let those who oppress the poor tremble.
The God of heaven and earth is righteous.
Let those who stray return to the Lord.
The Eternal Judge is seated in the judgment chair.
Let those who love justice shout for joy.
The Holy One rules.
Let us worship.

Opening Prayer (Matt 2)

Glorious God,
grant us the courage to follow Christ's natal star,
wherever your light would lead us;
grant us the wisdom to follow the kings of old,

as they left the safety of their homes
to find the infant Jesus;
grant us the purity of heart,
to forsake the glitter of things that do not endure,
and embrace the brightness of your glory.

—*Or*—

Opening Prayer (Isa 60, Ps 72, Eph 3, Matt 2)
God of starlight, disperse the darkness of our lives,
that we may behold the light of your love
shining in every corner of our world.
Guide our footsteps in the paths of righteousness,
that justice may flourish and peace may abound.
Help us follow the kings of old,
that through our own journeys of faith,
we may behold the mystery made known
through the coming of your glory
in the infant Jesus. Amen.

Proclamation and Response

Prayer of Confession (Matt 2)
Eternal God, following only a star in the sky,
kings of old left their families and their lands
to find a child whose birth was so profound,
it was proclaimed in the heavens above.
When we would rather sit comfortably in our homes
than make spiritual pilgrimages of our own,
clothes our feet of clay in walking shoes
and send us on our way.
At this season of light,
help us shine your light in the darkness

to honor the King of kings.
Open our shut-up hearts to those in need,
that the gifts of gold, frankincense, and myrrh
might not be the last gifts offered to the one
who brings light into our lives. Amen.

Assurance of Pardon (Matt 2, Eph 3)

The power that brought light and salvation
to the kings of old is at work in the world today,
granting eternal life to those who turn to God.

Passing the Peace of Christ (Matt 2)

Bathed in the light of God, turn to one another and ob-
serve the light that shines within each and every one
of us. Warmed by the light of Christ, greet one another
with signs of peace.

Response to the Word (Ps 72)

Let justice roll down like waters,
and righteousness like an ever-flowing stream.
Let the voice of the needy be heard throughout the land,
and the plea of the widow be answered.
Let God be praised and Christ proclaimed,
and let the whole world see the glory of our God.

—*Or*—

Response to the Word (Ps 72, Eph 3)

The word of God brings righteousness.
Let the sinner repent and return to the Lord.
The justice of God is stronger
than the foundation of the earth.
Let those who oppress the poor tremble.

The light of God shines the glory of our salvation
into the darkness of our lives.
Let all those who love God shout for joy.

Thanksgiving and Communion

Offering Prayer (Ps 72)
Merciful God, may your justice roll down like waters,
your righteousness like an ever-flowing stream.
May these gifts and offerings be an answer to your call—
a call to deliver the needy, rescue the weary,
and defend the poor and the defenseless.
In the holy light of your redeeming love, we pray. Amen.

Sending Forth

Benediction (Isa 60, Ps 72)
Go forth as a light to the nations.
We go forth, following the star of Christ's birth.
Go forth as a people of blessing.
**We go forth, proclaiming hope
to the poor and needy.**
Go forth as a light to the nations.
We go forth, with God's blessings.

—Or—

Benediction (Matt 2)
Follow the kings of old in search of God's Son.
We go with the promise of new life in Christ.
Follow the magi in search of meaning and purpose.
We go with the promise of new life in Christ.

January 12, 2020

Baptism of the Lord

Mary Scifres

Copyright © Mary Scifres

Color

White

Scripture Readings

Isaiah 42:1-9; Psalm 29; Acts 10:34-43; Matthew 3:13-17

Theme Ideas

Being chosen is a powerful theme, not just for today's readings, but for all of life. God has chosen each of us for different purposes and different paths; we have been chosen from the moment God created us. Today is not just a day to celebrate Jesus's baptism; this is a day to remember that we are all baptized, blessed, and called by God. We are all God's beloved, and God is pleased when we recognize and respond to our creation and our call.

Invitation and Gathering

Centering Words (Isa 42, Matt 3)

What if we recognized the image of God within us? What if we celebrated that we are God's beloved from the beginning of our existence? What if we claimed being chosen and destined for a loving purpose? How would we live and respond?

Call to Worship (Gen 1, Matt 3)
Created in God's loving image,
   we gather as the children of God.
Beloved by Christ, who loves us well,
   we gather as the beloved body of Christ.
Blessed by the Spirit of God,
   we gather in the power of the Holy Spirit.

Opening Prayer (Matt 3, Acts 10)
Beloved God, we gather as your beloved community
      in the name of your beloved Son, Christ Jesus.
Speak to us with your love and your grace.
Part the clouds of our frantic, harried lives,
      that we may recognize your Spirit
         moving in our very midst.
Speak, for your servants are listening. Amen.

Proclamation and Response

Prayer of Confession (Isa 42, Matt 3, Acts 10)
Beloved God, who calls us together in love,
      even as we rejoice in your love,
         we ask that you strengthen our love
            for one another.
Embolden us to love our adversaries
      and be kind to those who wrong us.
Cover us with your amazing grace,
      that we might love ourselves,

despite all of our misgivings, self-doubts,
and wrongdoings.
Guide us to live in your mercy,
that we may remember our baptismal call,
and live as those who are chosen and beloved.
In your mercy and love, we pray. Amen.

Words of Assurance (Matt 3, Acts 10)
You are God's beloved—forgiven, washed clean,
and ready to respond to this sacred truth:
You are chosen by God to love one another
as you have been loved.

Passing the Peace (Matt 3)
As beloved children of God, let us share signs and greetings of love with other beloved children in our midst.

Words of Preparation (Isa 42, Matt 3)
The things of old have passed away. God is always doing a new thing, calling us forth to claim our place as
chosen and beloved children. Listen, for God has something new to say today, just as God has new things to
say each and every day.

Thanksgiving and Communion

Offering Prayer (Ps 29)
Glory and strength are yours, O God.
May these gifts be offerings of glory and strength,
bringing the glory of your love,
and the strength of your grace,
to those who need them most.
In your precious name, we pray. Amen.

Sending Forth

Benediction (Isa 42, Matt 3)

Beloved children of God, we were created to love.
Blessed children of God, we were created to bless.
We go forth to love and bless God's world.

January 19, 2020

Second Sunday after the Epiphany
James Dollins

Color
Green

Scripture Readings
Isaiah 49:1-7; Psalm 40:1-11; 1 Corinthians 1:1-9;
John 1:29-42

Theme Ideas
This week's scriptures beckon us to see and share the
light of Jesus Christ. For those in the northern hemi-
sphere, our days are growing longer. At the same time,
Isaiah invites us to expand God's light and share it with
all nations. The psalmist has already shared glad news
with the congregation. Paul's words of praise teach us
how to encourage and expand Christ's love among us.
And John's Gospel invites us to "come and see" God's
light for ourselves and then share it with others, for
God's light is too good not to share!

Invitation and Gathering
Centering Words
Come, see and be seen.
Come, know and be known.

Understanding lends light to the eyes
    and peace to the heart.
Come to God, who knows you
    and calls you to love.

Call to Worship (Ps 40)
    I waited patiently for the Lord.
    God inclined to me and heard my cry.
        God drew me up from the pit,
        and made my steps secure.
    God put a new song in my mouth,
    a song of praise to our God.
        Many will see and believe,
        and put their trust in the Lord!

Opening Prayer (Isa 49, John 1)
    Author of creation, Maker of all that is,
        by your hands the seasons turn
            and the days grow longer.
    As sunlight expands irresistibly into dark corners,
        shed your light into our hearts,
            and into our world.
    Renew our spirits,
        that we may reflect your goodness
            to all who are alone or discouraged.
    Renew your Church, Holy Spirit,
        that we may worship and service
            with the joy of Jesus Christ,
                in whose name we pray. Amen.

Proclamation and Response

Prayer of Confession (Isa 49, John 1, 3:19)
    Precious Lord, you are the light
        who has come into the world.

Forgive us, when we love darkness
more than we love your light.
Keep us from dwelling on our weakness, foibles,
and fears.
Guard us from looking for darkness in others
rather than seeking the beauty that lies within.
Give us eyes to see you,
and grant us hearts to follow your Spirit,
that we may shine with the light of Christ. Amen.

Words of Assurance (John 1:5)
Hear the good news: God's light shines in the darkness
and the darkness cannot overcome it.
**In the name of Jesus Christ, we are forgiven.
Amen.**

Response to the Word (Isa 49, Lord's Prayer)
It is not right, says the prophet,
to seek the light of God's love for ourselves alone.
**We are called to bring light to all people,
until God's love reaches the ends of the earth.**
Let us seek the face of Christ in many different faces,
until God's love reaches the ends of the earth.
**Let us seek the divine in each neighbor we meet,
until God's love reaches the ends of the earth.**
Come, share the unique light God shines within you,
until God's love reaches the ends of the earth.
**May it be so on earth, as it is in heaven.
And may God's justice reign,
as God's will is done. Amen.**

Offering Prayer (Isa 49, John 1)
Dear God, Source of light and love,
all things belong to you.

You generously share with us
    the blessings of home, food, friends,
        and the gift of life.
Receive and bless these offerings,
    though they are but a portion
        of what you have given us.
May our gifts and joyful service
    strengthen your church in its efforts
        to share good news and compassion
           with everyone we meet.
This we pray, in Jesus's name. Amen.

Sending Forth

Benediction (Isa 49, John 1)
    Go in peace, and choose light over darkness,
        hope over despair,
    Go in the sure knowledge that God's goodness
        is all around us.
    Amen.

January 26, 2020

Third Sunday after the Epiphany

B. J. Beu
Copyright © B. J. Beu

Color

Green

Scripture Readings

Isaiah 9:1-4; Psalm 27:1, 4-9; 1 Corinthians 1:10-18;
Matthew 4:12-23

Theme Ideas

Themes of light and darkness focus the readings from
Isaiah, Psalm 27, and Matthew's Gospel. In the midst of
loss (destruction of one's homeland, the death of John
the Baptist), hope is not lost. God's light shines in the
darkness: "The people who walked in darkness / have
seen a great light; those who lived in a land of deep darkness— / on them light has shined" (Isa 9:2 NRSV).

Invitation and Gathering

Centering Words (Ps 27)
The Lord is our light and our salvation. Whom shall we
fear?

Call to Worship (Isa 9, Ps 27, Matt 4)

    The Lord is our light and our salvation.

        Whom shall we fear?

    The Lord sets us high on a rock, above our enemies.

        The Lord shelters us in our day of trouble.

    We, who have walked in darkness,

    have seen a great light.

        We, who have dwelled in a land of deep darkness,

        on us, light has shined.

    The Lord is our light and our salvation.

        Whom shall we fear?

Opening Prayer (Isa 9, Ps 27)

    God of radiant Light,

        shine into our lives,

            and disperse the darkness

                that dims our vision;

        shine into our world,

            and cast out the fears

                that long have chained us;

        shine into our worship,

            that we may be a people

                of your hope and promise. Amen.

Proclamation and Response

Prayer of Confession (Ps 27, Matt 4)

    Glorious God, our Light, and our Salvation,

        too often we have been afraid.

    We behold the beauty of your dwelling place,

        and feel unworthy to meet you there.

    We view the cleft in the rock,

        where you would hide us from our enemies,

            and we shrink from its dizzying height.

When your prophets are arrested and put to death,
> we hide in the darkness,
>> rather than proclaim the dawning
>>> of your great light.

Forgive our foolishness.
Guide our timid feet, O God,
> and do not turn your face from us, Amen.

Words of Assurance (Isa 9)

The gloom and grief of the former times
> have passed away.

The hope and glory of the latter times
> have washed over us like the tide of the sea.

We, who once sat in darkness,
> behold the glory of God's holy light.

Find joy and forgiveness
> in God's saving grace and redeeming love.

Passing the Peace of Christ (Isa 9)

As the body of Christ, we no longer walk in darkness, for we have seen a great light in this fellowship. See the light of Christ in those around you as you share signs of Christ's peace.

Response to the Word (Isa 9, Matt 4)

Radiant Light, shine into our hearts,
> that we might dwell in darkness no longer.

Summoning Word,
> guide our footsteps in the ways of life,
> that our lives might reflect your Word made flesh.

Draw us from the shadow of death
> into the dawning of your glory,
>> through the light we find in Christ Jesus. Amen.

Call to Prayer (Ps 27)

Seek the One who shines light into our darkness.
Trust the One who is the stronghold of our lives.
Call on the One who breaks the rod of the oppressor
    and brings warmth and light in the midst of winter.
(A time for silent prayer or Prayers of the People may follow.)

Thanksgiving and Communion

Offering Prayer (Isa 9, Matt 4)

Gracious God, we thank you for this day—
    a day blessed with light and joy,
    a day blessed with hope and abundance.
May these gifts bring light to those lost in darkness,
    and chase away the shadow of death
        from those who have lost hope.
Bless our lives to your service,
    in the name of the true Light. Amen.

Sending Forth

Benediction (1 Cor 1)

Go as people of Light.
    God's light shines upon us.
Go as people of Love.
    Christ's love shows us the way.
Go as people of Spirit.
    God's Spirit leads us home.
Go with God.

February 2, 2020

Fourth Sunday after the Epiphany
Karen Clark Ristine

Color

Green

Scripture Readings

Micah 6:1-8; Psalm 15; 1 Corinthians 1:18-31;
Matthew 5:1-12

Theme Ideas

Today's scriptures focus on states of being or doing. How shall I come before the Lord? How must I live my life if I am to abide in the tent of the Lord? Is it better to be wise in the eyes of the world or a fool for God? Finally, from the Gospel: What about the times when I feel poor in spirit? Blessed! What about when I am mourning? Blessed! Persecuted for my faith? Blessed! No matter our state of being, we seek right relationship with our creator.

Invitation and Gathering

Centering Words (Mic 6, Matt 5)

Come as you are, assured that you dwell in the blessings of the Lord. Open yourself to holy wisdom. Prepare yourself for humble service.

Call to Worship (Mic 6)

The Lord does not require your sacrifice.

We will be a people who lives justly.

The Lord does not need rivers of toil.

We will offer loving kindness to the world.

The Lord does not ask you to ignore your loved ones.

We will walk humbly with our God.

Opening Prayer (Ps 15, 1 Cor, 1 Matt 5)

Gracious and holy presence,

no matter our state of being,

you are with us.

When we mourn,

you call us blessed.

When we yearn for righteousness,

you call us blessed.

When we worry that we might be fools for our faith,

your wisdom guides our lives.

Open our minds and our lives this day

to your manifold blessing.

In the blessings of your presence,

may we speak your truth from grateful hearts.

Amen.

Proclamation and Response

Prayer of Confession (Mic 6, 1 Cor 1)

We confess, Holy One,

that in our human foolishness,

we often seek to appear wise.

Help us know the wisdom of your ways

and the truth of your Word.

We confess, Spirit Guide,

that we often fail to acknowledge your presence,
    seeking to go our own way,
        and following our own call.
From this centeredness on self,
    we let you down,
    we let others down,
    we let ourselves down.
Help us follow your direction, your call,
    and your guidance.
Help us to do justice, love kindness,
    and walk humbly with you. Amen.

Words of Assurance (Mic 6, 1 Cor 1)

No matter how you come before the Lord,
    the wisdom of the Holy One will be with you.
Your being overflows with the very forgiveness
    that will allow you once again walk humbly
    before our God.

Introduction to the Word (Mic 6, 1 Cor 1)

Listen for the wisdom of God, as we enter the Word.
Pray for understanding, as we invoke loving kindness
    and justice into living Word.

Response to the Word (Mic 6, Ps 15, 1 Cor 1, Matt 5)

We seek to do what the Lord requires.
We long to dwell in God's presence.
We honor the wisdom of the one who created our minds
    and our lives.
We are grateful, in all things and at all times,
    to be called blessed.
May we be a blessing to the Lord and to the world.

Thanksgiving and Communion

Offering Prayer

Ever-present and holy God,
we offer these gifts
in the hope that they will bring justice
to those in need;
we consecrate these gifts,
with the prayer that they will help others
learn to love in kindness
and to walk in humility.
Through these gifts to the world,
may those who hunger and thirst for righteousness
find blessing,
and may those who mourn for the state of the world
find peace. Amen.

Communion Prayer

Lord, may our hearts and minds and souls
be filled with the grace we receive at your table.
In our serve, may we help others
know your presence and your blessing. Amen

Sending Forth

Benediction (Mic 6)

Aware of the presence of God, our creator,
who loves each of us as we are;
aware of the grace of Christ, our redeemer,
who calls us blessed;
aware of the presence of the Holy Spirit,
who guides our lives—
go out in truth; go out in wisdom;
go out in love: to do justice, love kindness
and walk humbly in the presence of God.

February 9, 2020

Fifth Sunday after the Epiphany
Mary Sue Brookshire

Color

Green

Scripture Readings

Isaiah 58:1-9a (9b-12); Psalm 112:1-9 (10);
1 Corinthians 2:1-12 (13-16); Matthew 5:13-20

Theme Ideas

In Judaism, there is a notion called "*tikkun olam*" which is often translated "the repair of the world." According to Jewish tradition, there are divine sparks of light scattered throughout creation, and when we act with justice, righteousness, and kindness, the light shines and the world is healed. In this light-filled Epiphany season, today's texts from Isaiah, Psalms, and Matthew remind us that our light shines when we follow God's commandments and are "merciful, compassionate and righteous" (Ps 112:4b).

Invitation and Gathering

Centering Words (Isa 58, Ps 112, Matt 5)
> True worship leads us from reflection to action. God calls us to raise our voices and shine our lights as people of justice, mercy and peace.

Call to Worship (Isa 58, Ps 112, Matt 5)
> Come and see! God's light is shining brightly.
> **God's light shines in us.**
> When we honor God's commandments,
> **God's light shines in us.**
> When we feed the hungry and give to those in need,
> **God's light shines in us.**
> When we show mercy and compassion,
> **God's light shines in us.**
> We are the light of the world!
> **God's light shines in us. Amen.**

Opening Prayer (Ps 112)
> Luminous God, we give thanks
>> for this Epiphany season of light.
> When fear casts shadows in our lives,
>> open our hearts to your radiance.
> Shine on us, shine in us,
>> and shine through us.
> Make us beams of justice, mercy and love,
>> that we may brighten your world. Amen.

Proclamation and Response

Prayer of Confession (Isa 58, Ps 112, Matt 5)
> Loving Creator, you have placed within us
>> the spark of your Divine Light.

As people of your justice and mercy,
> you cause us to shine.

We long to grow closer to you
> and to walk in your ways.

And yet, we usually do whatever we want.

We point fingers at others
> and serve our own interests.

We satisfy ourselves with an hour in worship each week
> when there is so much more you ask of us.

When we fail to heal your world,
> forgive us.

Give us hearts that are open, generous, and unafraid,
> that your divine spark might ignite within us
>> and make us shine as beacons of your kindness
>> and your love. Amen.

Words of Assurance (Isa 58)
> Even when we stray,
> **God continues to guide us.**
> Even when our souls are parched,
> **God provides for us.**
> Even when we call for help,
> **God says, "I'm here."**
> Praise God!

Passing the Peace of Christ (Matt 5)
> The light of God shines within us. As you greet one another with signs of Christ's peace, remind your neighbor: "God's light shines in you!"

Response to the Word (Isa 58, Matt 5)
> God's love satisfies our needs.
> **Like a spring that never runs dry,**
> **God waters the gardens of our souls.**

God's righteousness lights our path.
> **Like a lamp on a stand,**
> **God illuminates our hearts.**

God's justice calls us to care for others.
> **Let us be Menders, Restorers, Healers.**
> **We are the Light of the World.**

Thanksgiving and Communion

Invitation to the Offering (Isa 58, Ps 112)

God provides abundantly for us and calls us to give generously to those in need. With gratitude for the blessings we have received, let us offer our gifts so that others may be blessed.

Offering Prayer (Isa 58, Ps 112)

Gracious God, through these gifts, given freely—
> may the hungry be fed,
> > the homeless receive shelter,
> > > and the mistreated be set free.

We offer all we have and all we are,
> that your light might break forth in us. Amen.

Sending Forth

Benediction (Isa 58, Ps 112, Matt 5)

Shine, people of God, shine!
Do not hide your light.
Stand up and raise your heads.
Open your mouths, your minds and your hearts.
Take your worship out of these doors.
Be gracious, merciful, and righteous.
You are the light of the world. Shine!

February 16, 2020

Sixth Sunday after the Epiphany
Karin Ellis

Color

Green

Scripture Readings

Deuteronomy 30:15-20; Psalm 119:1-8; 1 Corinthians 3:1-9;
Matthew 5:21-37

Theme Ideas

In this season of Epiphany, today's scriptures remind
us of the blessing it is to choose the ways of God. In
these scriptures, we hear the invitation to follow God's
commandments. In Deuteronomy, we are instructed to
"choose life." The psalmist encourages us to be blameless and walk in the ways of God. Paul reminds us that
it is God who gives growth and empowers us to be servants. And Matthew offers us commandments to follow
that lead to life.

Invitation and Gathering

Centering Words (Matt 5)

When we say, "Yes" to God, we choose to follow God's
ways and to live as Christ lived. Today, let us say, "Yes!"

Call to Worship (Deut 30, Ps 119)

This is the day the Lord has made!

We come rejoicing and giving thanks.

This is the day God invites us to love and to live.

We seek to dwell in God's love
as we turn our hearts toward God.

This is the day to worship our creator and redeemer.

We worship the God of life.

Opening Prayer (Ps 119, 1 Cor 3)

Almighty God, we gather in this space
to praise your name.

Help us lay aside our worries, our fears, our frustrations,
and our anxieties,
that we may be free to truly worship you.

Through the power of your Spirit,
empower us to seek your ways,
walk in the footsteps of Christ,
come before you with our whole heart,
and live as your faithful servants.

We seek your help this day, O God,
that the world may know your abundant love
and your amazing grace.

In the name of Christ, we pray. Amen.

Proclamation and Response

Prayer of Confession (Deut 30, Matt 5)

Gracious God, there are so many times
when our hearts turn away from you:
when we become angry or judgmental;
when we speak falsehoods;
when we squander your blessings;
and when we covet the things that are not ours.

Forgive us.
Help us speak words of encouragement and love.
    and help us follow your ways,
        that we may be your faithful followers.
In your holy name, we pray. Amen.

Words of Assurance (Deut 30:15, 19 NRSV)

Our loving God has said,
    "I have set before you today, life and prosperity,
    death and adversity....Choose life."
Brothers and Sisters, in the name of God,
    you are forgiven.
Now, choose life, and turn your hearts toward God.
Amen!

Passing the Peace of Christ (1 Cor 3)

We are God's servants...
    working together to build the kingdom of God.
May the peace of Christ be with you.
    And also with you.

Prayer of Preparation (Deut 30, Ps 119)

Holy One, stir our sense of wonder and curiosity,
    that your holy word may come alive for us
        in new and wondrous ways.
Open our ears and our hearts
    to your word of life this day. Amen.

Response to the Word (1 Cor 3)

We have heard your word spoken.
Now, may that word grow in our hearts and our lives,
    that we may work together to build a world
    where all may share God's abundant life. Amen.

Thanksgiving and Communion

Invitation to the Offering (Deut 30)

God has blessed us with the gift of life. For the blessings
that come in our lives, let us offer our thanks and show
our gratitude to God through today's offering.

Offering Prayer (Deut 30)

God of abundant life, we give you thanks
for your many gifts.
Most of all, thank you for the gift of life
and for all the ways we are able to worship
and to serve you.
May these gifts bring abundant life
to those both near and far.
In your precious name, we pray. Amen.

Sending Forth

Benediction (Deut 30, 1 Cor 3)

Brothers and sisters, go forth and choose life.
Walk in the ways of Christ.
Be strengthened by the Holy Spirit,
that the world might know the love
and the peace of God.
Go in peace.

February 23, 2020

Transfiguration Sunday
James Dollins

Color

White

Scripture Readings

Exodus 24:12-18; Psalm 99; 2 Peter 1:16-21;
Matthew 17:1-9

Theme Ideas

God blesses us with high points in life, to help us bear
the lows. Like mountain peaks that attract our eyes and
lift up our heads, God's blazing light shines for Moses
on Mount Sinai, and through Jesus at his Transfiguration. In both cases, an unforgettable vision will help
God's sojourners find strength to endure future trials.
Second Peter includes a unique first-person account
of the Transfiguration, while Psalm 99 strikes a fitting
chord of awe and praise. May the mountaintop of this
Sunday enable us to traverse life's valleys and to pro-
ceed with courage as we enter Lent.

Invitation and Gathering

Centering Words (Matt 17)

Transfigured by light, Jesus was changed. All those who witness God's light will be changed. Climb to the mountaintop to see God and to see yourself bathed in God's holy light. Climb to be changed.

Call to Worship (Ps 99)

Come, praise the Lord our God,
and worship at God's mountain.
For the Lord our God is holy,
full of compassion and grace.
When God's prophets cried out, God answered them,
speaking in a pillar of cloud.
Let all God's people sing praises
to God's great and awesome name.
Mighty God, lover of justice,
you establish equity throughout the earth.
Let us worship God from the mountaintops.
Let us praise God's holy name.

Opening Prayer (Matt 17, 2 Pet 1)

Light of God, shine upon us in this hour.
We come to you as we are,
in our strength and in our weakness.
Bless our world, in all its beauty and its pain,
with your Spirit's redeeming power.
As you transfigured Jesus on a mountaintop,
transform us as we worship you today.
Touch us with the presence of your Spirit,
that we may shine Christ's light
into a world longing for peace. Amen.

Proclamation and Response

Prayer of Confession (Exod 24, Matt 17, 2 Pet 1)
Gracious God, we have seen your light and glory
in the work of your church,
in the faces of loved ones,
and in the life of Jesus Christ.
Yet our memories are short,
and we complain if we no longer feel
your presence among us.
Forgive us when we descend from life's mountaintops
and turn our minds from the knowledge
of how you have loved us.
Pardon us when we neglect to seek you
in the faces of lonely and suffering neighbors.
Open our eyes and our ears, Lord.
Teach us to seek you always,
and to listen to the call of your call.

Words of Assurance (Exod 24, Matt 17, 2 Pet 1)
The light of God's grace shines upon us and through us.
Knowing us completely, God accepts and loves us still.
In the name of Jesus Christ, we are forgiven.
Amen.

Response to the Word (Matt 17) *pastoral*
(*Looking ahead to Lent*)
From the mountaintop, we gain perspective,
a rare panoramic view.
All is well in the presence of God,
where love and forgiveness reign in our hearts.
"It is good for us to be here," we say to ourselves,
wishing that we could stay.

But others need to climb this mountain,
    as they long for God's love to find them.
Our journey has only begun.
    Precious Lord, let us walk with you
        as you have walked with us—
            to mountaintops, through low valleys,
                to the cross and to life eternal,
                    through the grace of Jesus Christ,
                      our Lord. Amen.

Offering Prayer (Exod 24, Matt 17)
Generous God, you reveal your goodness and light
    through countless blessings and gifts.
Receive our offerings—
    a small portion of what you have given us—
        and reveal your goodness and grace to others
            in the name of Christ, our Lord. Amen.

Sending Forth

Benediction (Exod 24, Matt 17, 2 Pet 1)
Let us not linger too long on this mountain.
Go and bear God's light to a world that longs for peace.
May God our Creator, Redeemer, and Comforter,
    walk with us now and forevermore.
    Amen.

February 26, 2020

Ash Wednesday
Bryan Schneider-Thomas

Color
Purple

Scripture Readings
Joel 2:1-2, 12-17; Psalm 51:1-17; 2 Corinthians 5:20b–6:10; Matthew 6:1-6, 16-21

Theme Ideas
Our Ash Wednesday scriptures focus on repentance and preparation. Ash Wednesday is the invitation to undergo a forty-day Lenten journey—a journey of preparation that culminates in the Triduum (the three days beginning on Holy Thursday), and the Easter celebration. The call to repentance is the beginning of this journey. Creating an atmosphere of reflection and devotion serves the intent of Ash Wednesday, as does providing time and space for individual reflection and confession.

Invitation and Gathering

Centering Words
God sounds an alarm and calls us together. God hears our cries and heals our brokenness.

Call to Worship (Joel 2)
>Come, young and old ...
>Sanctify yourselves before the Lord.
>>**We gather to hear the word of God.**
>Come, and do not delay....
>Return to God.
>>**We gather to be in the presence of God.**
>Come, cry out to God....
>Trust in God's mercy.
>>**We gather to renew our spirits,**
>>**as we acknowledge our failings before God.**

Opening Prayer (Joel 2)
>We turn to you, God of life,
>>on this first day of Lent,
>>>as we recall our own mortality.
>With hearts torn open by our actions,
>>we need your guidance
>>>and your healing forgiveness.
>Ready us to receive your mercy and grace,
>>and cleanse us of the ash of human failing,
>>>that we may embrace the words your speak—
>>>>words that lead to eternal life. Amen.

Proclamation and Response

Prayer of Confession (Ps 51)
>In preparation, present yourselves before God.
>Come in your brokenness,
>acknowledging where you have fallen short
>of God's expectations and of your own.
>*(Time of silent reflection.)*
>Have mercy on me, O God,
>>according to your steadfast love.

The brokenness that hinders me,
I lay before you.
Come in your pain, acknowledging your hurt
and accepting how you have hurt others.
(Time of silent reflection.)
Do not cast me away from your presence,
 and do not take your Holy Spirit from me.
All the pain I have in my life—
  the pain I have caused and the pain I feel—
  I lay before you.
Come in your weakness,
acknowledging your lack of confidence
to do what is right.
(Time of silent reflection.)
Have mercy on me, O God,
 according to your steadfast love.
The weakness that holds me captive,
 I lay before you.
Come in your fear,
acknowledging your failure to seek justice.
(Time of silent reflection.)
Do not cast me away from your presence,
 and do not take your Holy Spirit from me.
The fear that binds me,
 I lay before you.
Come in your hesitancy,
acknowledging your resistance to God's call.
(Time of silent reflection.)
Have mercy on me, O God,
 according to your steadfast love.
My hesitancy in doing your will,
 I lay before you.

Come in your failings,
acknowledging what you have done and left undone.
(Time of silent reflection.)
Create in me a clean heart, O God,
    and put a new and right spirit within me.
      The hollowness that saps my strength
        and leaves me lifeless,
          I lay before you.
All that we are, all that we have done,
    all that we confess, we lay before you, O God.
    Relieve the weight of the burden,
      I lay before you. Amen.

Words of Assurance (Joel 2)
    Joel reminds us that God is gracious and merciful,
      slow to anger and abounding in steadfast love.
    With great mercy, God relents from punishing
      and calls us into fullness of life.
    In God's grace, know that you are forgiven.
      In God's grace, know that you are forgiven.
    In God's mercy, know that you are made new.
      In God's mercy, know that you are made new.
    In God's love, know that you are made whole.
      In God's love, know that you are made whole.

Introduction to the Word (Ps 51, 1 Cor 5)
    We entreat you on behalf of Christ,
    be reconciled to God.
      Speak, O Lord, and we will listen!
      In our inner most hearts,
      may your wisdom dwell.

—Or—

Introduction to the Word (Ps 5, 1 Cor 5)
Hear the word of God.
Speak to us the word!
We listen with open hearts
and contrite spirits.

Response to the Word (Ps 5, 1 Cor 5)
Together, we have heard the word of God.
Accept God's grace, that its telling was not given in vain.
Create in us a clean heart, O God,
and put a right spirit within us.

Thanksgiving and Communion

Invitation to the Offering
(This may be an opportunity to collect an offering other than money. You may wish to invite people to write their sins, confessions, Lenten commitments, or other appropriate words on small slips of paper. Give instructions early in the service to give the congregation time to think, pray, and respond. Collect the slips and offer them to God. If time, space, and safety permit, burn the paper and use the ash later in the service for the imposition of the ashes.)
Tonight our offering to God is a written sign of our *sins/ confessions/commitments*. Place these signs in the offering plate as it passes. The God of grace and mercy will hear your cry.

(Alternatively, if you are encouraging people to take on a Lenten discipline, this is a good time to pass out tokens of this discipline, such as a pocket cross.)
Typically, our offering to God focuses on the money we give, but tonight (today) we ask you to look at your

offering as your gift of time and spiritual reflection over the next forty days. During these days, I invite you to take on a Lenten discipline—a devotion to God. As a reminder of this offering, take a token of this discipline from the offering plate and carry it with you throughout Lent.

Offering Prayer

Almighty God, we come before you tonight
    to offer you far more than our money.
We offer our very lives to you,
    as a living sacrifice.
We offer our naked and honest selves,
    for you delight not only in praise,
        but also in repentance.
We offer our failings and faults,
    for you desire not only glory,
        but also confession of our sorrow
        and our sin.
Lord of Life,
    take the whole of our offering this night,
        for you have the power to make it beautiful
        and whole in your sight. Amen.

Introduction to the Imposition of Ashes
(2 Cor 5:20b–6:1 NRSV)

The apostle Paul writes:
"We entreat you on behalf of Christ,
    be reconciled to God,
    for our sake [God] made him to be sin
    who knew no sin,
    so that in him we might become
    the righteousness of God.

As we work together with him,
>we urge you also not to accept
>the grace of God in vain."

Ash is a traditional sign of repentance and contrition.
Tonight, the mark of the cross
>is made upon your foreheads in ash
>as a sign of our desire to be reconciled with God.

Come before God.
>**We come confessing our failings.**

Come before God.
>**We come acknowledging our need.**

Come before God.
>**We come facing our mortality.**

Come before God.
>**We come ready to receive God's forgiveness**
>**and fullness of life.**

Imposition of Ashes (2 Cor)

(Make the sign of the cross with ashes upon the forehead of each worshiper. Traditionally, the palms from the preceding Palm Sunday are burned to create the ash. Ash may be mixed with olive oil to facilitate the process, but should not be mixed with water. You may wish to provide the option to kneel while receiving the imposition. The person making the mark may use these or similar words:)

"Remember that you are dust
>and to dust you will return."

>—or—

"Repent and believe in the gospel."

>—or—

"Marked with the cross, be reconciled to God."

>—or—

"From the ashes of repentance, God brings new life."

Sending Forth

Benediction

With the ash of repentance, we have entered Lent.
With contrite hearts, we await our Lord.
Go forth and make preparations
to receive the power of God.

March 1, 2020

First Sunday in Lent

B. J. Beu

Color

Purple

Scripture Readings

Genesis 2:15-17; 3:1-7; Psalm 32; Romans 5:12-19;
Matthew 4:1-11

Theme Ideas

Today's scriptures highlight the reality of temptation
in human life. Adam and Eve succumbed to temptation, whereas Jesus did not. Whether or not we accept
Paul's suggestion that death entered the human condi-
tion through Adam's transgression, most Christian theologians posit that we have the power to avoid our own
temptations. To avoid robbing this Sunday of its theological depth, we must take seriously scripture's claim that
Jesus was tempted by the devil in the wilderness: Feeding people is good. Demonstrating God's power to rescue
us is good. Having Jesus rule the world with righteousness would be good. But focusing on these goods would

have kept Jesus from his higher purpose. The temptation
to choose a lesser good because it is easier than pursuing
a great good is something we all can relate to.

Invitation and Gathering

Centering Words (Matt 4)

Temptations surround us every day. Even Jesus felt its
pull in the wilderness. But when we keep our focus on
God's call in our lives, we find the strength to move beyond its pull—we find the resources to move toward
greatness.

Call to Worship (Ps 32, Matt 4)

Happy are those whose transgressions are forgiven.
Happy are those who receive God's mercy.
Rejoice and be glad, you upright in heart.
Shout for joy, you people of God.
Let us worship the one who gives us strength
to resist temptation in the wilderness of our lives.

—Or—

Call to Worship (Gen 2, 3; Rom 5)

Forbidden fruit is such a delight to the eye.
God is our delight.
Forbidden pleasures tug at us each day.
God is our joy.
Temptation is everywhere.
We can live as God intends,
through Christ who strengthens us.
Let us sing to the Lord,
who saves us from the time of trial.
Sing to the Lord, our delight and our joy.

Opening Prayer (Matt 4)

Walk with us, faithful traveler,
 as we journey with Christ
  through the season of Lent.
Help us overcome the temptations we face
 each and every day.
Save us from the time of trial,
 and send your angels to minister to us
  in times of weakness.
Raise us to newness of life,
 through the gift of your Spirit
  and the love of your Son. Amen.

Proclamation and Response

Prayer of Confession (Matt 4)

Holy One, we do not always face temptation well.
We settle for loaves of bread
 when our souls long for bread
  that does not perish.
We put you to the test,
 seeking signs of your favor,
  when we should "be still"
   and rest in the knowledge
    that you are God.
We place our trust in leaders
 who make promises they cannot deliver,
  when we should be putting our faith in you.
Forgive us, O God,
 and help us be found worthy of your calling,
  through Jesus Christ, our Lord. Amen.

Words of Assurance (Ps 32, Rom 5)
> When we acknowledge our failings before God,
>> God wipes away our shame.
> Receive forgiveness and mercy,
>> through the gift of God's grace in Christ.

Passing the Peace of Christ (Rom 5)
> Christ's justifying love brings peace to those who love God. Turn to one another and share the wondrous gift of God's peace in Christ.

Response to the Word (Ps 32)
> God has taught us the way we should go.
> Do not be like horses or mules,
>> dumb beasts without understanding
>> that must be curbed with bit and bridle.
> Rather, let us turn to God freely,
>> and rejoice in the one who leads us into life.

Thanksgiving and Communion

Offering Prayer (Matt 4)
> Holy One of Israel, work through these gifts.
> As we provide loaves of bread for the hungry,
>> work through our offering,
>>> that others may be fed,
>>>> not only in body, but in spirit.
> As we seek to bring justice to our world,
>> may we embody faith in your righteous love,
>>> that your people may know
>>>> the source of their hope. Amen.

Sending Forth

Benediction (Ps 32, Matt 4)
    Though life is full of temptation,
    God will see us through.
        We rejoice in the one who strengthens us.
    Though life is full of times of trial,
    Christ walks with us every step of the way.
        We rejoice in the one who shares our journey.
    Though life is full of obstacles to faith,
    the Spirit eases our burden.
        We rejoice in the one who leads us home.
    Go with God.

March 8, 2020

Second Sunday in Lent

B. J. Beu
Copyright © B. J. Beu

Color

Purple

Scripture Readings

Genesis 12:1-4a; Psalm 121; Romans 4:1-5, 13-17; John 3:1-17

Theme Ideas

The readings from Genesis and the Gospel of John speak of God's blessings, that we might be a blessing to others. If Abram will set out in faith, God promises to bless those who bless him, and to curse those who curse him (Gen 12:3). And John assures us that God's Son was not sent into the world to condemn the world, but to save it (John 3:17). How can our response to God be anything less than extending that blessing to others? Psalm 121 makes it clear that the one who helps us and keeps us from evil is the same God who created the heavens and the earth.

Invitation and Gathering

Centering Words (Gen 12)

Listen, for God is calling. Follow, and you will never be alone.

Call to Worship or Benediction (Gen 12)

The God of Abram leads us forward.
Lead on, O God…guide us home.
The God of Abram is here to bless us.
Bless us, O God, that we might be a blessing.
The God of Abram leads us forward.
Lead on, O God…guide us home.

—*Or*—

Call to Worship (Gen 12)

Leave your well-worn paths and walk with God.
But we are secure where we are.
Walk in new paths and you will be blessed.
Can't God bless us on our own turf?
If you will walk in faith,
God will bless those who bless you,
and curse those who curse you.
Lead on, O God,
your faithful people await.
Receive God's blessing to be a blessing to others.

Opening Prayer (John 3)

Loving God, you delight in showing us your kingdom—
a place of blessing,
a place of light,
a place of Spirit and truth.
May we be born anew in your Spirit,

that we might see the glory
you have in store for us
and for the world.
For you sent your Son into our world,
not to condemn us or put us to shame,
but that we might be have life,
and have it abundantly. Amen.

Proclamation and Response

Prayer of Yearning (Ps 121, John 3, Gen 12)
Maker of heaven and earth,
lift our eyes to the hills,
that we might find our help
in times of trial.
Like Nicodemus before us,
we long to lift our gaze from the ground
and behold your blessed face
calling us to follow you.
Like your disciples of old,
we yearn to set fear aside
and to be found faithful
in the presence of your awesome power.
Teach our hearts anew to trust your Spirit
and the promise of your blessings. Amen.

Words of Assurance (Gen 12:2 NRSV)
Hear the words spoken by God to Abram,
as if they were spoken to us as followers of Christ:
"I will make of you a great nation,
and I will bless you, and make your name great,
so that you will be a blessing."

Passing the Peace of Christ (Gen 12)

As Abraham before us, we are blessed by God, that we might be a blessing to others. Turn to those around you and offer words of blessing and peace.

Response to the Word (John 3, Gen 12)

Eternal God, your Spirit moves through us
    like an ever-flowing stream.
Your word, like the wind,
    blows where it will,
        blessing a weary world
            with newness of life.
Reside in our hearts this day,
    that we may be born from above
        and reside in your grace.
Revive our spirits,
    that we might be blessed
        to be a blessing to others. Amen.

Call to Prayer (Ps 121)

The one who made heaven and earth is listening.
The one who keeps your soul is ready to hear your plea.
The one who saves you from all evil
    awaits your prayers of thanksgiving and petition.
Lift up your eyes to the hills,
    behold the one who is your help,
    and offer up your prayers to God.
(A time for silent prayer or Prayers of the People may follow.)

Thanksgiving and Communion

Offering Prayer (Gen 12)

Gracious God, just as you blessed Abram
    when he ventured out in faith,
        you have blessed us with so much.

Help us see our gifts and offerings,
>not as fruit of our hard work,
>>but as blessings we have received
>>>from your generous hand.
In grateful response to our many blessings,
>we offer you these offerings,
>>that they may bless a world in need. Amen.

Sending Forth

Benediction (Ps 121:5-8 NRSV)
Hear the words of the psalmist.
>"The Lord is your keeper.
>The Lord is your shade at your right hand.
>The sun shall not strike you by day,
>>nor the moon by night.
>The Lord will keep you from all evil.
>God will keep your life.
>The Lord will keep your going out
>>and your coming in
>>>from this time on and forevermore."
Go with the blessings of God.

March 15, 2020

Third Sunday in Lent

Mary Scifres
Copyright © Mary Scifres

Color

Purple

Scripture Readings

Exodus 17:1-7; Psalm 95; Romans 5:1-11; John 4:5-42

Theme Ideas

We thirst for God, and God's presence is always with us, ready to quench our thirst. In each of today's readings, God is ready and waiting, present and available. The Israelites doubted God's presence and felt parched, as did the Samaritan woman, and perhaps even the church at Rome. Even so, God's grace was right there—as it always is—ready and waiting to quench our troubled souls and nourish us with life ever after.

Invitation and Gathering

Centering Words (Exod 17, John 4)
You, who are thirsty, come. Here, you will find Christ's grace to quench your thirst, and God's love to nourish your souls.

Call to Worship (Ps 95, John 4)

Let's sing to God,

for God is here.

Let's sing of love,

for love is here.

Let's sing and rejoice,

for here our souls are restored.

Opening Prayer (Exod 17, John 4)

Ever-present God,

even as you are present with us this day,

we yearn to feel your presence in our midst

each and every day of our lives.

Speak to us with words of grace.

Reveal yourself with the power of your love.

Flow over us with the presence of your Holy Spirit.

Help us know the glory of your love

and experience the wonder of your grace.

In the name of your love, we pray. Amen.

Proclamation and Response

Prayer of Confession (Exod 17, John 4)

Faithful One, we long to trust

your steadfast faithfulness.

We yearn to know your life-giving love.

Love us into faithful living.

Wash over us with your grace.

Nourish us with the water of your presence,

and lead to eternal life.

In the name of your love, we pray. Amen.

Words of Assurance (John 4)

Christ, the Living Water, is here,
>washing over us with mercy,
>>and filling us with hope and renewal.

Rejoice and be glad,
>for we are renewed with love
>>and made whole with grace.

Response to the Word (John 4)

Come to the table of grace,
>**for grace meets us here.**

Trust the love of God,
>**for God's love fills us now.**

Rest in the presence of Christ,
>for Christ meets us here.

Thanksgiving and Communion

Offering Prayer (John 4)

Living God, through these gifts we now bring,
>help our world live.

Loving God, through these gifts we now bring,
>help our world love.

Nourish others as you have nourished us,
>with your steadfast presence
>>and your healing grace. Amen.

Sending Forth

Benediction

Blessed by God's love
>and strengthened by Christ, our Living Water,
>we go to bless God's world with love.

March 22, 2020

Fourth Sunday in Lent
Karen Clark Ristine

Color

Purple

Scripture Readings

1 Samuel 16:1-13; Psalm 23; Ephesians 5:8-14;
John 9:1-41

Theme Ideas

Right call. Right path. Right light. Right timing. Each passage this week references God-ordained rightness. God's call of a leader might look different from tradition. The path of the Lord as Shepherd is the path of righteousness. When God illuminates our way, we are children of light, seeking what is good and right and true. When the Lord works miracles in human lives, the timing belongs to God, not the arbitrary calendars of humanity. Step into God's timing and God's view. Hear God's call and follow the path set by the Lord.

Invitation and Gathering

Centering Words (1 Sam 16, Ps 23, John 9)

Show me your way, O God, my Shepherd. Open a right
path and let me hear your call to follow. Show me your
way, O Christ, my Healer. Open my eyes to the needs of
my world.

Call to Worship (1 Sam 16, Ps 23, Eph 5, John 9)

Shepherd us, O God.
Open our ears to hear your calling.
Shepherd us, O God.
Open our eyes to see your care.
Shepherd us, O God.
Shear our fascination with the ways of the world.
Shepherd us, O God.
Prepare us to follow you.

Opening Prayer (Ps 23, John 9)

Visionary creator, give us your vision.
Show us our hearts, our homes, our communities,
    and our world through your eyes.
Wash away our blind spots,
    and help us to see where we do not see.
Allow us to see creation as you see it now,
    and as you envision it to become.
Help us realize your vision,
    and walk the road of life—
        the way and path of Jesus. Amen

Proclamation and Response

Prayer of Confession (Eph 5, John 9)

Divine God, our Guide, give us the clarity
    to wake to our short-sightedness and stay woke.

Give us the courage to wake to our shortcomings
and stay woke.
Give us the compassion to wake to our hurtful acts
and stay woke.
Give us wisdom to face our fears, receive your grace,
wake to your call and stay woke.
Hear our silent prayer,
as we sit in awareness of our need.
(Pause in silent prayer)
Help us wake to this awareness and stay woke.
As we receive your grace,
we wake to your whispers and direction,
yearning to stay woke. Amen.

Words of Assurance (Eph 5:14 NRSV)
"Sleeper, awake! Rise from the dead,
and Christ will shine on you."
**"Sleeper, awake! Rise from the dead,
and Christ will shine on you."**

Prayer of Preparation (1 Sam 16, Ps 23, Eph 5, John 9)
Open our mind's eye, Holy One.
Prepare our hearts to receive your call in our lives,
through the word we hear proclaimed.
Wake us to your truths.
Use your word to set us along the right path this day.
May the meditations of our hearts
be pleasing and acceptable to you.

Response to the Word (1 Sam 16, Eph 5, John 9)
We hear you calling Holy One.
We sense your healing presence, Light of Christ.
We will follow the path you illuminate, Great Spirit.

Thanksgiving and Communion

Offering Prayer (Eph 5, John 9)
God of our waking, receive these monetary gifts,
that they may bring the goodness of our ministry
to your world.
Receive also the gifts of our transformed lives,
as we open our hearts
to perceive our short-sightedness.
Give us the vision to offer our lives
in service of you.
Light our paths, and shine through our lives,
as we follow you. Amen.

Sending Forth

Benediction (1 Sam 16, Ps 23, Eph 5)
Go forth, woke to the call of God, your creator.
Go forth, true to the path lit by Christ, your redeemer.
Go forth, woke to the conscience of the Holy Spirit,
your helper and guide.

March 29, 2020

Fifth Sunday in Lent

B. J. Beu

Color

Purple

Scripture Readings

Ezekiel 37:1-14; Psalm 130; Romans 8:6-11; John 11:1-45

Theme Ideas

From the valley filled with dry bones in Ezekiel, to the death of Lazarus in John, today's theme focuses on experiences of loss and death, and the hope of new life in God. We feel dried up, devoid of breath, aching from the loss of loved ones, but death and loss do not have the final word. We worship a God who brings new life and new visions. We place our hope in a God who has power even over death. What have we to fear? With Paul, we know that: setting the mind on the Spirit is life and peace. Lent is a time to choose life.

Invitation and Gathering

Centering Words (Ezek 37)

When our lives feel like a valley of dried bones, the Spirit clothes our hearts with flesh and breathes new life into our souls.

Call to Worship (Ezek 37)

When our lives become a valley of dry bones,
> **God clothes us with flesh**
> **and hearts that beat with love.**

When our souls seem withered away,
> **God breathes new life into us once more**
> **that we might live.**

Come! Let us worship.

–Or–

Call to Worship (Ezek 37, John 11)

Behold a miracle.
> **A valley full of dry bones**
> **is transformed into a people of love and life.**

Behold a miracle.
> **The graves are opened.**
> **Death has lost its sting.**

Come and worship the one who never forsakes us!
> **Let us worship the Lord.**

Praise Sentences (John 11)

Praise the Lord of life!
Praise the one who brings us back from the grave!
In Christ we will never truly die.
Praise the Lord of Life!

Opening Prayer (Ezek 37)

God of promise and hope,
>we come to you feeling dried up,
>>like a valley filled with dry bones.

Share your visions of new life with us,
>that we might have hope for our future.

Bring us up from the grave,
>that we might live as people of promise.

Put your Spirit within us,
>that we might have life everlasting. Amen.

Proclamation and Response

Prayer of Confession (John 11)

Lord of life, we come to you
>consumed by our worry and our pain.

When we blame you for not being there in our need,
>forgive us.

When we turn away from you in moments of loss,
>guide us back to your faithful arms.

For we long to put our faith
>in your promised healing.

We yearn to truly believe
>that you are the resurrection and the life.

Teach us once more, Merciful One,
>that you weep when we weep,
>>and rejoice as we find our way home. Amen.

Assurance of Pardon (Ezek 37:14 NRSV)

God makes us a promise:
>"I will put my spirit within you and you shall live."

The one who showed Ezekiel that a valley of dry bones
>could live again will bring us newness of life
>>through Christ, who is the resurrection and the life.

Passing the Peace of Christ

We are not a valley of dried bones, but a people of Spirit—a people of passion and vitality who draw strength from the one we follow. Let us share the joy of being alive as we pass the peace of Christ with one another.

Introduction to the Word (John 11)

Listen to the word of God,
for God's word is life.
But death runs swift.
Believe in the promise of the resurrection.
We want to believe,
help our unbelief.
Those who live and believe in Christ will never die.
We will find faith in the lord of life.

Response to the Word (Ps 130)

Our souls wait for the Lord,
more than those who wait for the morning.
More than those who wait for the morning.
Put your hope in the Lord!
We put our hopes in God's steadfast love.
God has great power to redeem our lives.
We turn to the one who heals us.

Thanksgiving and Communion

Offering Prayer (Rom 8)

Holy God, you sent your Son into the world,
that we might set our minds on life and peace,
rather than dwelling on earthly things.
Receive this offering,
that it may go forth to continue the work of Christ,
who brings fullness of life.

May our gifts be a source of light in a world
    that has learned to love the darkness. Amen.

Sending Forth

Benediction (Ps 130)
    Go with the blessings of the one
    who forgives our failings.
        We go with God's blessings.
    Go with the blessings of the one
        who saves us and heals our hearts.
        We go with God's blessings.
    Go with God.

April 5, 2020

Palm/Passion Sunday

B. J. Beu

Copyright © B. J. Beu

Color

Purple

Palm Sunday Readings

Psalm 118:1-2, 19-29; Matthew 21:1-11

Passion Sunday Readings

Isaiah 50:4-9a; Psalm 31:9-16; Philippians 2:5-11;
Matthew 26:14–27:66 (27:11-54)

Theme Ideas (Palm Sunday)

Palm Sunday presents worship planners with a quandary: to focus the entire service on Jesus's triumphal entry into Jerusalem, and risk moving from the joy of Palm Sunday to the joy of Easter without moving through the anguish of Holy Thursday and Good Friday; or to move quickly from the parade atmosphere of Palm Sunday into the turning of the crowds, the betrayal, and the passion narratives, and thereby risk losing attendance at the forthcoming Holy Week services. Since Easter makes no sense without Christ's passion and death, we will err on the side of including the passion events in today's service. Fickleness of heart and betrayal are themes in this day's service.

Invitation and Gathering

Centering Words (Matt 21)

On the back of a humble donkey, Christ looks beyond the shouts of "Hosanna in the highest." He is traveling a slow journey to the cross—and he will pay the price of turning the tables on the money changers, upsetting the status quo, and living authentically before God. Will he travel that road alone?

Call to Worship (Ps 118)

This is the day that the Lord has made.
Let us rejoice and be glad in it.
Blessed is the one who comes in the name of the Lord.
God's steadfast love endures forever.
The stone that the builders rejected
has become the chief cornerstone.
This is the Lord's doing.
It is marvelous in our eyes.
Bind the festival procession with branches.
Jesus is the gate of the Lord.
The righteous enter through him.
This is the day that the Lord has made.
Let us rejoice and be glad in it.

Opening Prayer (Matt 21, Phil 2)

Blessed One, we are humbled by your example.
You entered Jerusalem in lowly estate,
riding on a donkey.

You emptied yourself and came as a servant to all,
    forsaking the power to command.
Son of David, come to us now and be our King,
    that we too may sing our hosannas! Amen.

Proclamation and Response

Prayer of Confession (Matt 26–27)
God of righteousness,
    this day places a mirror before our faces.
We would rather sing hosannas
    with the cheering crowd,
        than stand up for our convictions
            in the face of an angry mob.
We would rather dine with Christ at his table,
    than stand up for him in a courtyard of accusers.
We would rather see ourselves as Christ's champions,
    than admit to ourselves that we too could betray
        him with a kiss.
Forgive our fickle faith,
    and heal our hesitant hearts.
In your loving name, we pray. Amen.

Words of Assurance (Ps 118)
God has opened the gates of righteousness,
    and the righteous enter through it.
The one who is our cornerstone,
    the stone the builders rejected,
    has become our salvation.
God offers us forgiveness and fullness of grace
    in Christ's name.

Passing the Peace of Christ (Matt 21)

Let us share with one another the joy of the Palm Sunday crowds, as we share signs of Christ's peace on this holy day.

Response to the Word (1 Pet 2)

Merciful God, we tremble when we think how easily
Judas betrayed you.
We shake at all the times we have denied you
like Peter before us,
through our words and our actions.
May your words live within us and strengthen us,
that we might keep our eyes focused on the cross
and walk with Christ to the end. Amen.

Call to Prayer (Ps 31)

Like broken vessels,
we need God' healing.
Like those who are dead,
we need the stirring of God's life within us.
Like an army surrounded by its enemies,
we need Christ's deliverance.
Let us lift up our prayers to God—
the one who delivers us from evil,
the one whose steadfast love
makes us whole again.

Thanksgiving and Communion

Offering Prayer (Gen 12)

Holy One, your love for us is so great
that you gave us your own Son
to teach us the ways of life and death.

May the gifts and offerings we bring this morning
reflect our gratitude for Christ's gift of self,
for Christ's anguish and passion,
and for Christ's never-failing love. Amen.

Sending Forth

Benediction (Ps 118)
The gates of righteousness are thrown wide.
We go with God's blessings.
The path of salvation is made plain.
We go in Christ's truth.
The cornerstone of our faith is sure.
We go with the Spirit's grace.
Go with God and walk with Christ
during this holy week.

April 9, 2020

Holy Thursday
Karin Ellis

Color

Purple

Scripture Readings

Exodus 12:1-4 (5-10) 11-14; Psalm 116:1-4, 12-19;
1 Corinthians 11:23-26; John 13:1-17

Theme Ideas

On this holy night, we remember, celebrate, and give
thanks to God. The psalmist invites us to worship with
thanksgiving and praise. Exodus recounts the story of
the Passover, and in the readings from 1 Corinthians
and the Gospel of John, we find the story of Jesus's last
supper with his friends. Common themes run throughout these stories. The Israelites make sacrifices on behalf
of God; Jesus foreshadows the sacrifice he will make on
behalf of humanity. The Israelites will receive a new beginning as they are led from slavery to freedom—a covenant based on unconditional love through the death
and resurrection of Christ. Jesus will serve his friends
and invite them to become servants of one another.

These scriptures invite acts of remembrance and celebration, that we may give thanks for God's abundant
providence, abiding presence, and unconditional love.

Invitation and Gathering

Centering Words
In the dark of the evening, guided by candlelight, we
come to remember and give thanks.

Call to Worship (1 Cor 11, John 13)
We have gathered in the dark of night
to remember and give thanks.
We have gathered around the Lord's Table
to hear stories of our faith,
feast on the Word made flesh,
and proclaim God's abundant love!

—Or—

Call to Worship (Ps 116, John 13)
In the dark of the evening, guided by candlelight,
we come to remember and give thanks.
In the solemnness of this hour, guided by prayer,
we come to worship, to be fed by God's Spirit,
to be filled with Christ's amazing love.

Opening Prayer (Ps 116)
Gracious God, we have been called here
by your inviting Spirit.
As we come to worship and praise your name,
we wonder: "What can we bring you?"
In the dark of night, and in the depths of our hearts,
we hear your reply:
"Your love is all I require."

So, in thanksgiving and praise,
    we bring you our whole selves,
        with hearts full to bursting.
Incline our ears to your word,
    and open our hearts to the mystery
        of this holy night. Amen.

Proclamation and Response

Prayer of Confession (Exod 12, John 13)
Holy Lord, on this night of mystery,
    we ask with the disciples,
        "Lord, do you seek to wash our feet?"
It is hard to witness acts of selfless service,
    for our actions are rarely pure.
Forgive our selfish tendencies.
Forgive us when we fail to live by your example.
Help us listen for your guidance,
    and overcome our shortcoming,
        that we may become your faithful servants. Amen.

Words of Assurance (John 13:34 NRSV)
Brothers and sisters, hear these words of Christ:
    "Just as I have loved you,
    you also should love one another."
We are loved and forgiven and free,
    and made ready to once again
    share God's grace with one another.
Thanks be to God!

Passing the Peace of Christ (Exod 12)
As families and friends, we are invited to celebrate
God's presence with one another. Let us greet one an-
other with the peace and spirit of Christ.

Introduction to the Word (1 Cor 11)

May the words of my mouth,
>   **and the reflections of our hearts,**
be received with grace,
>   **and celebrated with joy.**

Response to the Word (1 Cor 11, John 13)

Holy One, we give thanks for your word,
>   which has been with us this day.
Help us remember the lessons you teach—
>   that through brokenness
>   we find healing and new life;
>   and that through the waters of grace
>   we find cleansing and rebirth.
May these words be written on our hearts,
>   and shared with the world,
>   that all may come to know
>   your love and your grace. Amen.

—*Or*—

Response to the Word (Ps 116, John 13)

Jesus said, "Just as I have loved you, love one another."
My friends, be filled with the love of Christ.
>   **The love of Christ flows through us**
>   **and around us. Praise the Lord!**

Thanksgiving and Communion

Invitation to the Offering (Ps 116)

We have been called by God to offer our prayers, our presence, our hearts, and our gifts. In response to God's generous love, let us offer what we can with thanksgiving and praise.

Offering Prayer (Exod 12)
> Loving God, we give you thanks and praise
> > for the gifts you have given us.
> May these gifts be used to spread your love
> > and your grace with those in need—
> > > those who are in exile,
> > > those who are hurting,
> > > > and all who are in need of your touch.
> May these gifts be a celebration
> > of your very presence. Amen.

Great Thanksgiving
> Christ be with you.
> > **And also with you.**
> Lift up your hearts.
> > **We lift them up to God**
> Let us give our thanks to the Holy One.
> > **It is right to give our thanks and praise.**

> It is a right, good, and a joyful thing
> > always and everywhere to give our thanks to you,
> > who led the Israelites out of bondage into freedom,
> > who commanded them to keep the Passover
> > as a remembrance of how you saved their firstborn
> > from death, and how you brought them out
> > of the land of Egypt.

> And so, with your creatures on earth
> > and all the heavenly chorus,
> > we praise your name
> > and join their unending hymn, saying:
> > **Holy, holy, holy One, God of power and might,**
> > > **heaven and earth are full of your glory.**

**Hosanna in the highest. Blessed is the one
who comes in your holy name.
Hosanna in the highest.**

Holy are you, and holy is the Lamb of God,
    Jesus Christ, who taught us how to love
    and serve one another,
    and who poured out his life
    for the healing of the world.
On the night in which he gave himself up
(continue with the Words of Institution)...
    do this in remembrance of me.

And so, in remembrance of your mighty acts
    in Jesus Christ...we proclaim the mystery of faith.
    Christ has died.
    Christ is risen.
    Christ will come again.

Pour out your Holy Spirit on all of us gathered here,
    and on these gifts of bread and wine.
Make them be for us the body and blood of Christ,
    that we may be the body of Christ,
        in service to all who are oppressed.
God of Moses and Miriam and Aaron,
    God of Exodus and Calvary,
        God of memory and hope,
            we praise your holy, eternal name.
    Amen.
(Deborah Sokolove)

Sending Forth

Benediction (John 13)
>   Brothers and sisters, remember this night.
>   Remember the broken bread, the shared cup,
>   and the cleansing water.
>   Go into this night
>   remembering and celebrating
>   Christ's presence among us.
>   Go in peace! Amen.

April 10, 2020

Good Friday
Shelley Cunningham

Color

Black or None

Scripture Readings

Isaiah 52:13–53:12; Psalm 22; Hebrews 10:16-25;
John 18:1–19:42

Theme Ideas

We live in a world that needs Good Friday now as much
as ever. Estrangement, injustice, violence, despair, and
war are but signs of our broken relationships with God
and with one another. In this service of Tenebrae, the
worship space becomes increasingly darkened, signifying that our movement away from God comes, not
with a sudden rejection, but with small steps: one de-
nial, one betrayal, one insult, one lash at a time. Some
of these steps wound God's people, and in so doing,
pierce God's heart. In naming our missteps and our
own part in Christ's death, we understand how much
we need this day—a day to fathom the depth of God's
love for us.

Invitation and Gathering

Centering Words (John 19)

Darkness is falling. Our journey ends here, at the foot of your cross. Our journey ends where love comes to die.

Call to Worship (John 19)

When we are lost and lonely,
Jesus, remember me.
When worry threatens to crush our spirits,
Jesus, remember me.
When our words wound the people we love,
Jesus, remember me.
When we treat others with contempt and disdain,
Jesus, remember me.
When we come into God's kingdom,
Jesus, remember me.
Welcome me home.

Opening Prayer (John 19)

Lord, our journey ends here,
at the foot of the cross.
Darkness is falling.
The crowd is restless.
Our hearts break,
as your cries pierce the night.
Stay with us, Lord,
for we need you close at hand.
And when the night is over
and the journey continues,
give us the courage to stay with you.
Amen.

Litany of Confession (Isa 53, John 19)

Surely he has borne our infirmities
and carried our diseases.
I am the one who held the nails.
We accounted him stricken,
struck down by God, and afflicted.
I am the one who raised the hammer.
But he was wounded for our transgressions.
I am the one who rolled the dice.
He was crushed for our iniquities.
I am the one who pointed and laughed.
Upon him was laid the punishment that made us whole.
I am the one for whom he died.
By his bruises, we are healed.
When I know not what I do,
do not withhold your love,
for we long to be made whole.

Words of Assurance (Heb 10)

Even as he hung on the cross,
Jesus spoke words of love.
To the thief, to his tormentors,
to a world of sinners, our Lord says:
"I will remember your sins no more."
For you, Jesus carried that cross.
For you, Jesus bled and died.
For you, Jesus spoke words of love.
For you, Jesus offers forgiveness and grace.

Proclamation and Response

(Place seven candles on a bare altar. After each word, scripture, and response is read, extinguish one candle. It is powerful

to accompany the extinguishing of each candle with the ringing of a single bell and a slight darkening of the sanctuary or worship space. The sayings of Jesus are adaptations; the response is Isa 53:6 NRSV.)

Tenebrae Liturgy

FIRST WORD:

> "Father, forgive them,
> for they know not what they do."

(Read Luke 23:32-38)

And we, like sheep, have gone astray.

We have all turned to our own way.

(Extinguish first candle)

SECOND WORD:

> "Today, you shall be with me in paradise."

(Read Luke 23:39-43)

And we, like sheep, have gone astray.

We have all turned to our own way.

(Extinguish second candle)

THIRD WORD:

> "Woman, mother, behold your son."
> "Behold your mother."

(Read John 19:23-27)

And we, like sheep, have gone astray.

We have all turned to our own way.

(Extinguish third candle)

FOURTH WORD:

> "My God, my God, why have you forsaken me?"

(Read Matthew 27:45-49)

And we, like sheep, have gone astray.

We have all turned to our own way.

(Extinguish fourth candle)

FIFTH WORD:
"I thirst"
(Read John 19:28-29)
And we, like sheep, have gone astray.
We have all turned to our own way.
(Extinguish fifth candle)
SIXTH WORD:
"It is finished."
(Read John 19:30)
And we, like sheep, have gone astray.
We have all turned to our own way.
(Extinguish the sixth candle)
SEVENTH WORD:
"Father, into your hands I commit my spirit."
(Read Luke 23:44-49)
And we, like sheep, have gone astray.
We have all turned to our own way.
(Extinguish the seventh candle)

Thanksgiving and Communion

Invitation to Reflect on the Cross (Ps 22)
(During this time, invite worshipers to write down issues they wish to bring before God, and then come forward and place the written cards on a large wooden cross or on the altar.)
Our brokenness leaves us in need of God's love and grace. With arms spread wide, our Lord invites us to find healing and wholeness. Let us bring our brokenness before God, knowing that we are not forsaken.

Unison Offering Prayer (John 19)
What can we bring you today, Lord?
Your sacrifice is so great;

our gifts seem so meager.
Yet you open your arms to us
and accept us as we are.
Take our offerings and use them, Lord,
for the healing of your kingdom. Amen.

Sending Forth

(There is no benediction on Good Friday. Some congregations completely darken the sanctuary for a moment, removing even the eternal candle to signify the deep darkness that enveloped the world when Jesus died. Encourage worshipers to leave in silence.)

April 12, 2020

Easter Sunday

B. J. Beu

Color

White

Scripture Readings

Acts 10:34-43; Psalm 118:1-2, 14-24; Colossians 3:1-4;
John 20:1-18 (or Matthew 28:1-10)

Theme Ideas

The steadfast love spoken of by the psalmist has raised
Jesus from the dead. How will we recognize our risen
savior? Jesus calls each of us by name—a call to disci-
pleship and service. The hymn, "Christ the Lord Is Ris-
en Today" says it all. Everything else is commentary.
Yet, before we give ourselves over to Easter celebration,
our service can reflect the hopelessness and defeat that
Mary and the disciples felt as they came to the tomb.
Beginning the service in near darkness with the cross
still shrouded with the black cloth of Good Friday is an
effective way to capture the surprising truth that death
does not have the final word.

Invitation and Gathering

Centering Words

Even in the midst of our Good Friday grief, a sparrow sings in the garden, heralding the morning, as sunlight kisses the dewy grass.

Call to Worship (John 20)

Shout for joy.
> **The tomb is empty.**

Clap your hands.
> **Death is cheated.**

Dance and sing.
> **Christ is risen.**

Christ is risen indeed.

Call to Worship (John 20)

(Begin the service in near darkness, with only an unlit Pascal Candle and a cross shrouded in black cloth on the altar/Lord's Table. Have a lit votive and small taper hidden behind the Pascal Candle. Place a couple of Easter lilies or other flowers hidden from sight behind the altar/Lord's Table. As the responsive liturgy is read, have a lone liturgical dancer (Mary) approach the chancel with head bowed, carrying a jar symbolizing the anointing oils Mary would have brought to the tomb. As the reading begins, the pianist plays a somber, reflective melody.)

The night is far gone.

There is dew on the grass.

> **We walk with Mary to the tomb.**

(As the reading continues, have one or more angels dressed in billowing white garb come from the side and dance around Mary. Mary continues to grieve as if she cannot perceive them.)

Lost in our grief, we feel abandoned…alone…
unaware that angels minister to us.
(Pause and let the dancers continue to the tomb, which could be a simulated cave or large stone made out of papier-mâché.)
We weep with Mary,
for all hope seems lost.
The stone is rolled back.
Only his grave clothes remain.
Overcome by our loss, we feel abandoned…alone…
unaware that Angels minister to us.
(Change the music to a more hopeful mood. Mary begins to move with cautious hope.)
A flicker of hope ignites in the soul…
wavering in the wind…
challenging the triumph of darkness.
Yet, surely there is no cheating death?
Gently, lovingly, angels question our tears…
for God is stronger than death.
(One angel lights the Paschal Candle with the taper hidden behind it, while another undrapes the cross. If sanctuary lights are on a dimmer, bring them slowly up to full. The angel who lit the Pascal Candle lifts up an Easter Lilly or other flower arrangement from behind the altar and places it upon the Lord's Table.)
Out of the shadows of the tomb,
the light of Christ shines forth in glory,
overcoming the darkness of sin and death.
In the depths of our souls,
the light of Christ brings *us* back
to the land of the living.
(Mary can now see the angels, and they all dance together with joy.)

As the light of Christ dawns,
we find that we are not alone.
> **The light shines in the darkness**
> **and the darkness did not overcome it.**

Opening Prayer (Ps 118, John 20)

God of mystery and might,
> your wondrous love
>> always seems to catch us off guard.

We come to the tomb
> looking for death,
>> but find life instead.

As we behold the glory of our salvation,
> take us back to that moment of discovery—
>> when grief and loss gave way
>>> to a glimmer of hope.

Before we shout our alleluias,
> remind us of the moment
>> when despair was transported
>>> into glimpses of new possibilities.

In the holy awe of Easter morning,
> we take a moment of silent gratitude
>> that Christ calls each of us by name.

(Moment of silence.)
Shout it from the mountaintop:
> Christ is risen! Alleluia!

Christ is risen indeed.
(The prayer leads naturally into a hymn like: "Christ the Lord Is Risen Today.")

Children's Moment

Before the service, hide the Easter Lilies among the pews or choir loft. During the Children's Moment, send the youth on a hunt to find the flowers, and then use them to decorate the worship space.

Proclamation and Response

Prayer of Confession (Acts 10)

Receive our lament, Lord of Life,
    for during your final days,
        we turned away from you,
            even after you shared table with us,
                offering us the bread of heaven
                    and the cup of salvation;
    and in your hour of greatest need,
        we fell asleep while you prayed in the garden,
            even after you urged us to keep the faith
                to avoid the time of trial.
But we are here now, dearest friend,
    remembering what it cost you
        to know the joy we feel today.
May our lives reflect
    the depth of our gratitude
        to be known as your disciples. Amen.

Words of Assurance (Acts 10)

The one who raised Jesus from the dead,
    offers us life and forgiveness of sin.
Rejoice in Christ our savior,
    whose resurrection brings us life.

Passing the Peace of Christ (Ps 118, John 20)

> With joy beyond measure in the face of cruelty and
> death, let us share the triumph of love over hate as we
> share signs of Christ's peace this blessed day.

Response to the Word (Ps 118)

> God is stronger than death.
>> **Give thanks to the Lord, for God is good.**
> Christ is stronger than death!
>> **God's steadfast love endures forever.**
> The Spirit is stronger than death.
>> **Let everyone shout out:**
>> **God's steadfast love endures forever.**
> Give thanks to the Lord!
>> **God is stronger than death.**

—Or—

Response to the Word (Ps 118)

> This is the day that the Lord has made,
>> let us rejoice and be glad in it.
> For this is the day that Christ rose from the dead,
>> bringing life in his name.
> In Christ, God has opened the gates of righteousness,
>> that those who seek fullness of life
>>> may enter through it.

Thanksgiving and Communion

Offering Prayer (Acts 10)

> God of grace and God of glory,
>> pour your power on your people this day,
>>> that our lives may reflect
>>>> the gift we have received

through the resurrection of your Son.
Truly we see that you show no partiality,
offering abundance of life and fullness of grace
to all who turn to you in their need.
With deepest gratitude for your many gifts,
particularly the gift of your Son,
we offer you our tithes and offerings this day.
In the name of the resurrected one, we pray. Amen.

Sending Forth

Benediction (John 20)
From darkness and despair, we find hope and joy.
Christ is risen! We go forth in joy!
From doubt and betrayal, we find trust and faith.
Christ is risen! We go forth in faith!
From suffering and death, we find healing and life.
Christ is risen! We go forth to live!
Christ is risen. Christ is risen indeed.
Alleluia.

April 19, 2020

Second Sunday of Easter

B. J. Beu

Color

(White)

Scripture Readings

Acts 2:14a, 22-32; Psalm 16; 1 Peter 1:3-9; John 20:19-31

Theme Ideas

The epistle reading promises us an imperishable inheritance through the resurrection of Jesus Christ from the dead. Each reading, in its own way, makes the bold claim: The peace of God, the divine love that is our refuge and our strength, can never be taken from us. Even when we doubt, as Thomas did, we are challenged to embrace the good news of our imperishable inheritance.

P 397

Invitation and Gathering

Centering Words (Acts 2, Ps 16, 1 Pet 1)

All the doubt in the world cannot wash away our inheritance from God—an inheritance of love, refuge, and strength.

Call to Worship *(Acts 2, Ps 16, 1 Pet 1)*

Come into God's presence with joy.

In God, we have an inheritance
that is imperishable.

Come into God's presence with hope.

In Christ, we have an inheritance
that cannot be defiled.

Come into God's presence with longing.

In the Spirit, we have an inheritance
that never fades.

Come into God's presence with love.

In God, we have an inheritance
that brings new life.

Opening Prayer *(Acts 2, Ps 16, 1 Pet 1, John 20)*

God of signs and wonders,
breathe new life into us this day,
that our spirits may awaken
to the joy and the hope
of our glorious inheritance
through the living Christ.
Clear our vision, Holy One,
that we may see the promise of Easter
in the stirrings of this precious earth
and in the life energy
flowing through our bodies.
Help us find the faith to believe
where we have not seen,
that others may see,
in our living and our loving,
the glory of the risen Christ. Amen.

Proclamation and Response

Prayer of Confession (1 Pet 1, John 20)

Merciful God,
you come offering us peace,
but we hold onto our fears;
you come offering us faith,
but we cling to our doubts;
you come offering us a future filled with promise,
but we retreat to pleasant memories of the past.
We want to believe that you offer us an inheritance
that is imperishable, undefiled, and unfading.
We want to see ourselves as you see us.
We want to live as you would have us live.
We want to believe that life is stronger
than the death we see all around us.
Help our unbelief, O God,
that we may truly know and live
your gift of resurrection. Amen.

Words of Assurance (1 Pet 1, John 20)

The inheritance that God promises us
is imperishable, undefiled, and unfading.
Even when we are consumed by doubt,
God is always faithful.
Even when we lose our way,
God is able to find us and bring us home.
Even when we are at war with ourselves,
God is able to bring us peace.
Thanks be to God!

Passing the Peace of Christ (1 Pet 1, John 20)

When our minds churn like turbulent waters, Christ
comes to offer us peace. When our lives career out of

control like cars on a frozen highway, Christ comes to offer us peace. Christ is here now, offering us peace. With the Spirit of Christ within us, let us turn to one another and share signs of peace with one another.

Response to the Word (1 Pet 1, John 20)

Even though we have not seen the Lord,
we can still love God.
> **Even though we cannot touch God's hands,**
> **we can still believe.**

Gathered here as the body of Christ,
and seeing Christ's love in one another,
we can say without doubt:
> **We have seen the Lord!**

When we witness the hands that touch us
and behold the eyes that shine Christ's love and peace,
we can proclaim with faith:
> **My Lord and my God!**

Do not doubt but believe.

Litany (1 Pet 1, John 20)

Deeds of power, signs and wonders…
Christ has risen from the dead.
> **Blessed be the God of our Lord, Jesus Christ.**

Deeds of power, signs and wonders…
Christ is alive in the world!
> **Blessed be the source of our glorious inheritance**

Deeds of power, signs and wonders…
Christ brings us peace!
> **Blessed be the Spirit that makes us whole.**

Thanksgiving and Communion

Invitation to the Offering (Ps 16)

God is our chosen portion and our cup of blessing. Christ is our delight and our refuge from the storm. The Spirit has given us a goodly inheritance and blessed us with abundance. Let us share our gratitude for the grace we have received by giving freely to a world in need of Easter joy.

Offering Prayer (Ps 16, 1 Pet 1, John 20)

O God, our refuge and our strength,
>   we rejoice that you are our chosen portion,
>> you are our cup that overflows to eternal life.

As we celebrate your Easter miracle
>   of bringing life out of death,
>> we express our gratitude and joy
>>> for the new life budding within us
>>> and all around us.

Bless the gifts we offer you this day,
>   that they may bring hope and new life
>> to a world that clings even now
>>> to the illusion of death's victory
>>>> over the Lord of Life. Amen.

Sending Forth

Benediction (1 Pet 1)

Through Christ, God has given us a new birth
into a living hope.
>   **God has given us an inheritance**
>   **that is imperishable, undefiled, and unfading—**
>   **an inheritance protected by the power of God.**

Rejoice, therefore, even if for a while
we suffer various trials.
    For life is stronger than death,
    love is stronger than hate,
    joy is stronger than sorrow,
    and the promises of God are sure.

April 26, 2020

Third Sunday of Easter

Mary Scifres
Copyright © Mary Scifres

Color

White

Scripture Readings

Acts 2:14a, 36-41; Psalm 116:1-4, 12-19; 1 Peter 1:17-23;
Luke 24:13-35; John 4

Theme Ideas

"Stay with us," say the disciples on the road to Emmaus
to their unknown companion. In that invitation, and in
the breaking of the bread together, they recognize they
are communing with Jesus himself. When we stay with
God and God's word for long periods of time, amazing
things happen. Peter proclaims that new birth grows from
the seed of God's enduring word. God's word endures
in our lives, when we immerse ourselves in the hearing,
proclaiming, and living of that word. Stay with God, invite God to stay with you, and wait for amazing growth.
This is the gift we receive simply for sticking around long
enough for God to nourish our lives with new growth.

Invitation and Gathering

Centering Words (Luke 24)

> Christ is here, ready to be revealed. Watch and wait for the new growth that is coming.

Call to Worship (Luke 24)

> Stay with Christ,
> and Christ will stay with you.
> **Listen for God,**
> **and God will speak.**
> Seek the Spirit,
> and the Spirit will be revealed.
> **For the Spirit is already here,**
> **inviting us to stay.**

Opening Prayer (1 Pet 1, Luke 24)

> Eternal God, we are here,
> yearning to know you more fully.
> Stay with us as we worship this day.
> Reveal yourself in the words that are spoken,
> the songs that are sung,
> and the bread that is broken.
> Help us understand your truth,
> and embrace your life-giving power,
> revealed within your enduring word.
> In Christ's holy name, we pray. Amen.

Proclamation and Response

Prayer of Confession or Prayer of Yearning (1 Pet 1, Luke 24, John 4)

> Holy One, we long to recognize your presence,
> but the journey can be confusing.

In the midst of our confusion,
>reveal yourself with grace and love.

We yearn to hear your voice,
>but noisy distractions surround us daily.

Cut through the distractions that overwhelm us,
>and bring us the clarity of your wisdom.

We desire to touch the living water
>of your mercy and forgiveness.

Grant us this life-giving water
>and the power of your enduring word,
>>that we may know your forgiveness
>>each and every day.

In the name of the risen Christ, we pray. Amen.

Words of Assurance (1 Pet 1, Luke 24)

In the name of the risen Christ,
>we are forgiven and free.

In the power of God's enduring word,
>we are given new birth,
>and offered a community of resurrection and hope.

Passing the Peace of Christ (1 Pet 1)

Let us share signs of genuine affection and Christian love, as we pass the peace of Christ.

Introduction to the Word (1 Pet 1, Luke 24)

Listen for the word that stands the test of time.

Listen for the word that lives and moves among us.

Listen for the word that God is speaking to us this day.

Response to the Word (1 Pet 1, Luke 24)

We have called on God,
>**and God's word has been spoken in our midst.**

Christ has joined us here,
and will stay with us,
even as we depart from this time of worship.
The Spirit is moving in our lives,
revealing the truth of resurrection and life
through all that we say and all that we do.

Thanksgiving and Communion

Invitation to the Offering (Ps 116)
Let's keep our promises to God, as we offer our love to
God's world through our gifts today.

Offering Prayer (Luke 24)
Living Christ, bless the gifts we bring
with the power of resurrection and hope. Amen.

Invitation to Communion (Luke 24)
Come to Christ's table,
and Christ's presence will be revealed.
As we break the bread and take the cup,
let us discover what Christ will bring us this day.

Communion Prayer (Luke 24)
Risen Christ, be present at our table,
as you were with those disciples
on their way to Emmaus.
As we break bread with you,
reveal your presence to us.
As we take the cup,
nourish us with your wisdom.
Stay with us, O Christ, and bless this time
with the power of your Holy Spirit,
that we may experience resurrection anew.
Amen.

Sending Forth

Benediction (Luke 24)

Christ is risen

Christ is risen indeed.

Christ is with us.

Christ is with us indeed.

Go to share this good news with the world!

May 3, 2020

Fourth Sunday of Easter

B. J. Beu

Color

White

Scripture Readings

Acts 2:42-47; Psalm 23; 1 Peter 2:19-25; John 10:1-10

Theme Ideas

The shepherd that is revered by the psalmist is celebrated by John as both shepherd and gate for the sheep. We rejoice that Jesus our shepherd calls us each by name, and is the one who came that we may have abundant life (John 10:10b). This abundant life is described in Acts as a result of fellowship, breaking bread together, prayer, attention to the apostle's teachings, and sharing all things in common (Acts 2:42, 44). How far we have moved from that early paradigm of selfless giving! But when we return to our shepherd and guardian after going astray, we are healed and welcomed home (1 Peter 2:24-25).

Invitation and Gathering

Centering Words (Ps 23, John 10)

The Good Shepherd calls his sheep by name. Listen, for our shepherd is calling.

Call to Worship (Ps 23, John 10)

The Lord is our shepherd.
> **We are the sheep of Christ's pasture.**

The shepherd makes us lie down in green pastures.
> **In Christ, we dwell secure.**

The shepherd leads us beside still waters
and restores our souls.
> **We worship Christ, our shepherd, our gate.**

—Or—

Call to Worship

Do you need a guide?
> **The Lord is our shepherd.**

Do you need a doorway to new life?
> **The Lord is our gate.**

Do you need rest?
> **The Lord restores our souls.**

Do you need care?
> **The Lord is our shepherd.**

Come, let us worship.

Opening Prayer (John 10)

Loving Shepherd,
> we feel the wolves close at hand.

Gather us to yourself,
> that we might dwell secure in your ways.

Deliver us from evil,

that we might build a community
where all may dwell secure.
Mark our fellowship with study, prayer, communion,
and the sharing of our possessions
with those in need. Amen.

Proclamation and Response

Prayer of Confession (Ps 23, John 10)
Christ, our shepherd and gate,
we would rather chart our own course,
than be shepherded like sheep;
we would rather find our own way,
than see you as the Way;
we would rather be shepherds than sheep,
who are vulnerable and exposed.
Forgive us when we bleat our resistance,
as you guide us to higher pastures.
Be our gate, our way to safe havens,
where we can dwell with you secure. Amen.

Words of Assurance (Ps 23)
The one who anoints our heads with oil,
the one who feeds us while our enemies look on,
the one who delivers us from evil,
invites us to dwell in the house of the Lord forever.

Response to the Word (1 Pet 2)
Keeper of our souls, when we go astray,
help us return to you,
shepherd and guardian.
May the words we have heard resonate within us
like a drum in the valley,
and may its echo never fade. Amen.

Call to Prayer (Acts 2)

The early disciples devoted themselves to prayer,
the teachings of the apostles,
and sharing the bread of life.
They were a people of prayer,
who shared their joys and concerns,
their passions and sorrows,
with one another and with the Lord.
For burdens shared are burdens lessened,
and joys shared are joys enriched.
Come, let us follow their example
and lift up our prayers to God.

Thanksgiving and Communion

Offering Prayer (Gen 12)

Holy One, touch us with the awe
that came upon those early disciples,
as they beheld the signs and wonders
performed in their midst by the apostles.
May the gifts we offer this day
be a remembrance of their commitment
to share all things in common.
In Jesus's name, amen.

Sending Forth

Benediction (Ps 23, John 10)

The Lord is our shepherd.
We shall not want.
In pastures green, we rest secure.
Our shepherd leads us forth.
By still waters, we rest secure.
Our shepherd brings us abundant life.
Go with the blessings of our shepherd.

May 10, 2020

Fifth Sunday of Easter,
Festival of the Christian Home / Mother's Day
Mary Sue Brookshire

Color
White

Scripture Readings
Acts 7:55-60; Psalm 31:1-5, 15-16; 1 Peter 2:2-10;
John 14:1-14

Theme Ideas

On the day we celebrate the Festival of the Christian
Home, we might ask, "What is a home?" At its best it is a
place where we are nourished, protected, and equipped
to go out into the world. Today's texts remind us that
as Christians, we have a home, a refuge, and a fortress
in God. From that firm foundation, we become the living stones with which God builds a spiritual home for
all God's people. Jesus promises to show us the way to
God's house, where there is room for all—room to spare!

Invitation and Gathering

Centering Words (Ps 31, 1 Pet 2)
God is our rock, the foundation of our spiritual home.
We are living stones, used to build God's house.

Call to Worship (Ps 31, 1 Pet 2, John 14)

Welcome home, people of God.
> **We have come to find refuge**
> **in the shelter of God's care.**

Come and sit down.
There is room for everyone in God's house.
> **We have come to be nourished by God's word.**

We are God's own people,
and are precious in God's sight.
> **We have come to give thanks**
> **for God's faithful love.**

Opening Prayer (Ps 31, 1 Pet 2)

We gather today O God, our guide and guardian,
> remembering those who have nurtured us,
>> protected us, and helped us grow.

We give you thanks for homes that accept us
> and affirmed us as your precious children.

In the shelter of your healing love,
> fortify us as living stones,
>> and build us into a spiritual home
>>> where all are welcome.

In the name of Christ,
> our foundation and cornerstone, we pray, Amen.

Proclamation and Response

Prayer of Confession (Ps 31, 1 Pet 2)

Holy One, you are our fortress and our rock,
> the foundation on which all things are built.

You have made us one family and one people—
> a holy priesthood, precious in your sight.

Yet we often pursue our own plans
> and ignore your designs for our lives.

We reject those who are different from us,
    and build walls that separate us from each other
        and from you.
Forgive us, O God.
Tear down the barriers we have put up,
    and rescue us from our isolation.
Gather together the living stones of our lives
    and fashion us into a holy temple,
        transformed by the marvelous light
          of your mercy and grace. Amen.

Words of Assurance (1 Pet 2, John 14)

Don't be troubled.
When we ask for anything in Jesus's name,
    it will be done.
Celebrate God's mercy and forgiveness.

Passing the Peace of Christ (1 Pet 2)

As living stones, God uses us to build a home where all
are welcome. Greet one another with the peace of Christ
and say, "Welcome home!"

Prayer of Preparation (1 Pet 2)

Like newborn infants, our hungry spirits long to be fed.
And like a loving parent, O God,
    you nourish us with your mercy and your grace.
Open our hearts to the goodness of your word. Amen.

Response to the Word (1 Pet 2)

The master builder has plans for us.
God delights in using what the world has tossed aside.
No matter who we are, God uses us as living stones,
    the building blocks of God's kin-dom on earth.

Thanksgiving and Communion

Invitation to the Offering (1 Pet 2)

Loving God, you have made us your people, so that we may speak of your wonderful acts. With gratitude for all we have received, we have come to offer our gifts to you.

Offering Prayer (Ps 31, 1 Pet 2)

O God, our fortress and our rock,
may these offerings be acceptable to you.
In a world facing profound need,
they seem insignificant,
but we know that in your hands,
even small things become great.
Use these gifts, and use our very lives,
to make this world a home
where all are sheltered, nourished
and cherished. Amen.

Sending Forth

Benediction (Ps 31, 1 Pet 2)

Once we weren't a people,
but now we are God's people.
God's face shines on us.
God's faithful love saves us.
This news is too good to keep to ourselves.
Everywhere we go, we will share the good news
of God's amazing grace.

May 17, 2020

Sixth Sunday of Easter
Karen Clark Ristine

Color

White

Scripture Readings

Acts 17:22-31; Psalm 66:8-20; 1 Peter 3:13-22; John 14:15-21

Theme Ideas

The desire to be near our creator, through faith and prayer, is present in each of these scriptures. This is the one "in whom we live and breathe and have our being" (Acts 17:28 NRSV). God is present, even when we are unaware. God is present in the hearing of our prayers. God is present when we suffer for doing good. God is present in the Advocate, the Spirit of truth, when the world believes human lies. No matter where we are in our faith journeys, the Holy is present.

Invitation and Gathering

Centering Words (Acts 17, John 14)

The Spirit of truth dwells among us. Bask in this awareness. In the Lord, we live and breathe and have our being. Rest in this presence.

Call to Worship (Acts 17)

> God made the world and everyone in it.
> **Our life and breath come from God.**
> God made all nations under heaven.
> **We are all God's offspring.**
> Search for God in our time of worship.
> **When we search, we find God near.**

Opening Prayer (Acts 17, Ps 66, John 14)

> Hear our prayers, O God,
> > as we come to sing your praises.
> Bless us with your steadfast love,
> > in times of peace and in times of trial.
> Make your presence known to us this day,
> > for we seek to know you better.
> Enliven us with your Spirit of truth,
> > and increase our faith,
> > > even as we place our hope and trust in you.
> Amen.

Proclamation and Response

Prayer of Confession (Acts 17, Ps 66, 1 Pet 3)

> Sometimes, O God, your ways are a mystery to us.
> When we cry out in desperation,
> > we don't really expect you to hear our prayers.
> When we suffer for doing the right thing,
> > it just seems like par for the course.
> When we deny or doubt your presence,
> > forgive us, O God.
> Make your presence known to us,
> > and receive our prayers and praise,
> > > as those who long to feel your presence. Amen.

Words of Assurance (John 14)

> The Spirit of truth abides with you and will be with you.
> Because the Lord lives, you also will live.
> Love God and receive God's abiding love.

Introduction to the Word (Acts 17, John 14)

> Listen for the presence of God in the word. Listen for
> the presence of the Holy in your lives. Worship a God
> who makes known a love for all of humanity. See a God
> who sends help and hope. Open yourselves to the Spirit
> of truth.

Response to the Word (Ps 66, 1 Pet 3, John 14)

> We will love as the Lord loves us.
> We will testify to the presence of God,
> > through the Advocate, the Spirit.
> We will prepare ourselves for times of suffering.
> We will open our hearts in praise and thanksgiving.
> God hears our prayers and heeds our call.
> We are not rejected,
> > for we are loved.

Thanksgiving and Communion

Offering Prayer (Ps 66, John 14)

> God of love, you are present in all things.
> Be present to a hurting world in these gifts.
> Help us use this offering to create a community of love
> > and a place of belonging for all people.
> Help us reach those who seek,
> > and those who doubt.
> Use these gifts to help people know
> > the blessings of being your beloved children.

Sending Forth

Benediction (Acts 17, John 14)

Go in the name of God,
 the one who created all the nations of the earth.
Go in the name of Christ,
 the one who abides in love and abides in you.
Go in the name of the Spirit of truth,
 the one who advocates for you and guides you.
Amen.

May 24, 2020

Ascension / Seventh Sunday of Easter
Mary Scifres
Copyright © Mary Scifres

Color

White

Ascension Sunday Scripture Readings

Acts 1:1-11; Psalm 47; Ephesians 1:15-23; Luke 24:44-53

Seventh Sunday of Easter Scripture Readings

Acts 1:6-14; Psalm 68:1-10; 1 Peter 4:12-14; 5:6-11; John 17:1-11

Theme Ideas

Joy flows through our readings as the Easter season comes to a close—a vivid reminder that this is a season of joy and celebration. Christ is risen! Christ ascends to heaven. Even so, the Risen Christ is in our very midst, for we are the body of Christ, the resurrection community, called to rejoice together in loving community. We are a sign of God's glory for all to see. Surely, this is cause for joy to flow through our lives, just as joy flows through today's readings.

Invitation and Gathering

Centering Words (1 Pet 4, Luke 24)
>Be glad and rejoice, for in our joy, we reveal God's glory
>and Christ's loving presence.

Call to Worship (Luke 24)
>Rejoice and sing to God.
>>**We sing of the Risen Christ.**
>
>Clap your hands and shout with joy.
>>**We rejoice in the living God.**
>
>Celebrate this day.
>>**We celebrate with the Spirit who calls us here.**

*Opening Prayer or Prayer of Thanksgiving (Luke 24, Ps 47,
John 17, Ps 68, 1 Pet 4)*
>Holy God, we celebrate your presence this day.
>For the gift of resurrection,
>>we give you thanks and praise.
>
>For the gift of your ongoing presence in our lives,
>>we rejoice and sing.
>
>Overwhelm us with your presence here,
>>that we might be overwhelmed with joy.
>
>In joyous gratitude, we pray. Amen

Proclamation and Response

Prayer of Confession (1 Pet 4, John 17, Eph 1, Luke 24)
>Heavenly Christ, come down from on high to be with us,
>>even in our darkest hours.
>
>As you share in our suffering,
>>share your love in the midst of our shortcomings
>>>and our failings.

Raise us to new heights
>with your forgiveness and mercy,
>>that we may glorify you in all that we say
>>and in all that we do.
Enter into our sorrows with grace and hope,
>that we might be overwhelmed with joy.
In your holy name, we pray. Amen.

Words of Assurance (1 Pet 4, Eph 1, Luke 24)

The Risen Christ is here, restoring, empowering,
>and strengthening us.
We are established as God's beloved children,
>forgiven and made new in Christ's love.

Passing the Peace of Christ (1 Pet 1)

Joy to the world! Christ is risen and is in our very midst.
Let's greet one another with this joyous news.

Introduction to the Word (John 17, Luke 24, Ps 68, Ps 47)

These are holy words—words that reveal God's love, words that inspire our hope, and words that bring us joy. Listen for signs of love, hope, and joy in the reading of God's holy word.

Response to the Word (John 17, Luke 24)

We are witnesses,
>**and testify to Christ's resurrection in our midst.**
We are the body of Christ,
>**called to reveal Christ's glory and love.**
We may be the only face of Jesus that others will see.
>**We will radiate the love and joy**
>**we have found in Christ.**

Thanksgiving and Communion

Invitation to the Offering (Ps 68)

As God has showered abundant love and grace on us,
may we share gifts of love and grace with God's world.

Offering Prayer (Ps 68, 1 Pet 4, Ps 47)

With joy, we bring our gifts.
With joy, we offer our lives.
May the offering of our gifts and our very selves
bring joy throughout the world. Amen.

Invitation to Communion (Acts 1, Ps 47)

This is the table of life.
This is the table of joy.
All are welcome here.
Rejoice in this marvelous gift.

Communion Prayer (Acts 1, Easter, Pentecost)

Holy God, pour out your Spirit on us,
and make us united in devotion,
as you united those first disciples.
Raise our eyes to the skies above,
that we may recognize the Risen Christ.
And open our hearts,
that we may anticipate your presence
and your Spirit in our midst.
In joyous gratitude, we pray. Amen.

Sending Forth

Benediction (John 17, Luke 24)

Joy to the world!

   The Lord has come to earth.

Joy to the world!

   Christ has risen from death itself.

Joy to the world!

   Christ's glory is ours to share.

May 31, 2020

Pentecost Sunday

B. J. Beu

Copyright © B. J. Beu

Color

Red

Scripture Readings

Acts 2:1-21; Psalm 104:24-34, 35b; 1 Corinthians 12:3b-13; John 7:37-39

Theme Ideas

As Jesus's disciples huddled together in fear, the Holy Spirit entered their dwelling in rushing wind and tongues of fire. In that moment, the Church was born. Without Pentecost, the gospel would not have moved beyond that group of disciples huddled in the upper room. The Spirit that was promised to the prophet Joel is active in our world today, granting visions and dreams to our old and young alike. The power of God to create and renew life is the power of the Holy Spirit. We see this power in the psalmist's hymn of praise. We behold this power in Paul's discussion of adoption in Christ through the Spirit. And we see the promise of this power in Jesus, as he comforts his disciples before his death.

Invitation and Gathering

Centering Words (Acts 2)

There is no fear the Holy Spirit cannot overcome. There is no door the Spirit of grace cannot breach. This is good news indeed.

Call to Worship (Acts 2, Ps 104)

With rushing wind and holy fire...
Come, Holy Spirit, come.
With tongues of flame and hopes rekindled...
Come, Holy Spirit, come.
With visions birthed and dreams restored...
Come, Holy Spirit, come.
With spacious grace and depth untold...
Come, Holy Spirit, come.
With rushing wind and holy fire...
Come, Holy Spirit, come.

—*Or*—

Call to Worship (Acts 2, Ps 104, Rom 8)

Call upon God's holy name.
For in calling, we are saved.
Listen for the wind of the Spirit.
For in listening, we find new life.
Respond to the promises of Christ.
For in responding, we bring hope to our world.

Opening Prayer (Acts 2, 1 Cor 12, John 7)

Spirit of Pentecost, blow open the doors
of our shut up hearts.
Set our tongues free
to proclaim your praise.

Bless our youth with visions,
    and our elders with dreams.
Bestow our children with gifts of prophecy,
    and renew the faith of your people
        throughout the world.
Blow into our lives, once more, Holy One,
    and help us find the strength and courage
        to become the people you call us to be. Amen.

Proclamation and Response

Prayer of Yearning (Acts 2, Ps 104, 1 Cor 12, John 7)
Spirit of wind and flame,
    blow open the doors we erect
        to keep ourselves sealed off from your world.
We long to be set free from the fears that jail us
    and to be released from chains that bind us.
We yearn to draw near to your source of living water,
    and to drink deeply from its well.
We want to be cleansed in your holy fire,
    and to be driven into the streets
        by your winds of grace.
Come to us, and heal us once more, Mighty Spirit,
    that we may embrace your gifts
        in service to a world in need. Amen.

Words of Assurance (Acts 2, Ps 104)
When God breathes the Holy Spirit into our lives,
    the earth is renewed.
When God blesses us with gifts of this same Spirit,
    we too are renewed and made whole.
Rejoice, sisters and brothers,
    God's steadfast love endures forever.

Passing the Peace of Christ (1 Cor 12)

Renewed through the gifts of God's Spirit, let us share our visions and dreams of peace by exchanging signs of Christ's peace with one another.

Introduction to the Word (Acts 2, John 7)

Can a locked door keep the Holy Spirit from releasing us from our fears? Can a quaking spirit keep us from receiving the Spirit's gifts today? Can the Church be born again after two thousand years of inertia and indifference? Does the story of Pentecost have anything to say to us today? Listen for the word of God.

Response to the Word (1 Cor 12, John 7)

With the gifts of the Holy Spirit, may our hearts overflow with living water on this day of Pentecost, and on every day of our lives.

Thanksgiving and Communion

Invitation to the Offering (Ps 104, 1 Cor 12)

We worship a God who is with us to the end. When God opens her hand, we are filled with good things. When God closes his hand, our bodies return to the dust, and our breath returns to Spirit, who gave it. Let us share the bounty of our lives with God on this day of Pentecost.

Offering Prayer (Ps 104, 1 Cor 12, John 7)

For opening your hand,
> and blessing us with your manifold blessings,
>> we give you thanks, O God.

On this day of Pentecost,
> may our gifts bring dreams and visions

to world in need of hope and direction.
And may our hearts overflow
with rivers of living water. Amen.

Sending Forth

Benediction (Acts 2, Ps 104)

With rushing wind and holy fire,
go forth in the power of the living God.
We go forth as God's children.
With tongues of flame and hope rekindled,
go forth in the power of the eternal Christ.
We go forth as heirs with Christ.
With visions birthed and dreams restored,
go forth in the power of the Holy Spirit.
We go forth as new creations in God's Spirit.
With spacious grace and depth untold,
go forth in the mystery of the Holy One.

June 7, 2020

Trinity Sunday
Hans Holznagel

Color

White

Scripture Readings

Genesis 1:1–2:4a; Psalm 8; 2 Corinthians 13:11-13; Matthew 28:16-20

Theme Ideas

These readings remind us of the insight that the essence of God is relational. God speaks in first-person plural in the creation story (Gen 1:26). Paul emphasizes community (2 Cor 13:11-12). Jesus encourages baptism in the Triune name (Matt 28:19). The partners in God's creation—God's people—are "we."

Invitation and Gathering

Centering Words (Gen 1:26a, 31a NRSV)
"Then God said, 'Let us make humankind in our image, according to our likeness.'…God saw everything that God had made, and, indeed, it was very good."

Call to Worship (Gen 1, Ps 8, Matt 28)
>For the "many-ness" of God's creative splendor,
>>**let us give thanks.**
>Before Jesus's humility,
>and the power of Christ's commands,
>>**let us stand in wonder.**
>For the mystery of relationships—
>God's with us, and ours with one another,
>>**let us seek God's holy wisdom.**
>Come! Let us worship the Triune God.

Opening Prayer (Gen 1, Ps 8, Matt 28)
>You are One, O God, and you are Three.
>You are majesty and mystery.
>Make us ever in your image, we pray.
>Make us one.
>Make us "we." Amen.

Proclamation and Response

Prayer of Confession (Gen 1, Matt 28, 2 Cor 13)
>God of creation,
>>we often imagine we must go it alone.
>Remind us, at such moments,
>>of the "we" in your creation,
>>>the Three in our baptism,
>>>>and the "one another" in our community.
>Comfort and empower us,
>>as we gather in your Spirit. Amen.

Words of Assurance (2 Cor 13, Matt 28:20b NRSV)
>Jesus said, "I am with you always."
>Friends, seek earnestly to live in peace,

and know that the God of peace and love
is with you. Amen.

Passing the Peace of Christ (2 Cor 13)

Paul invites us to greet one another with a holy kiss. Perhaps today our greeting will be more formal. But with
equal warmth of spirit, please greet your neighbor with
a sign of God's peace.

Response to the Word (Gen 1, 2 Cor 13)

May the same Word that created all things
bear fruit in our lives, in the community of faith,
and in the world.

Thanksgiving and Communion

Invitation to the Offering (Gen 1)

In thanksgiving for the fruitful abundance of God's creation, let us give back a portion of what we have received.

Offering Prayer (Matt 28, Gen 1)

Gracious God, Holy Trinity,
we offer these gifts and ourselves
as instruments of your ever-new creation. Amen.

Sending Forth

Benediction (2 Cor 13:13 NRSV)

Hear these words of the ancient church:
"The grace of the Lord Jesus Christ,
the love of God, and the communion
of the Holy Spirit be with all of you."
Go forth to live in peace. Amen.

June 14, 2020

Second Sunday after Pentecost, Proper 6 / Father's Day

B. J. Beu

Color

Green

Scripture Readings

Genesis 18:1-15; Psalm 116:1-2, 12-19; Romans 5:1-8; Matthew 9:35-10:8 (9-23)

Theme Ideas

With God, all things are possible. These hopeful words in Matthew's Gospel ring throughout today's readings. Sarah laughs at the absurd idea of bearing a child in her old age, while Abraham is reminded that "nothing is too difficult" (Gen 18:14, "wonderful" in the NRSV) for God. Romans reminds us that we are saved by faith, not works, and God, therefore, gets the glory. Matthew tells us that humble disciples are given the power to cast out demons and cure illness. These myriad miracles of God offer us a hope that passes all understanding.

Invitation and Gathering

Centering Words (Gen 18, Matt 10)
> Laugh with Sarah, as life grows within the womb of an
> old woman. Stand in amazement with the crowds, as
> illiterate fishermen perform the miracles of God. Forget
> what you think you know. Expect miracles. For with
> God, anything is possible!

Call to Worship (Ps 116, Rom 5)
> Call to the Lord, who hears our prayers.
> **Sing to the Lord, who delights in our songs.**
> Wait for the Lord, the source of our hope.
> **Worship the Lord, who is worthy of our praise.**

Opening Prayer (Gen 18, Matt 10)
> God of wondrous love,
>> your miracles always catch us by surprise.
> When our time of blessing comes,
>> may we laugh with Sarah
>>> and dance with Abraham.
> When our bodies are touched by your healing grace,
>> may we bow before your throne of glory.
> Come to us now, as we gather to worship,
>> that we might be touched by your Spirit
>>> and made whole by your grace. Amen.

Proclamation and Response

Prayer of Yearning (Gen 18)
> Steadfast source of mercy and grace,
>> we long for you to touch our lives,
>>> as you touched the lives of Sarah and Abraham;

we yearn to laugh at blessings that are so unlikely,
    we can scarcely believe them;
we desire to feel in our very bones,
    that no problem we face is beyond your care.
Grant us the wisdom to put our trust in you,
    and to offer you our songs of praise
    and our shouts of joy. Amen.

Words of Assurance (Gen 18, Rom 5, Matt 10)
In God's faithfulness, we are made well.
In Christ's love, we discover righteousness and peace.
In the Spirit's sustaining power,
    we find strength for the journey.
Thanks be to God.

Passing the Peace of Christ (Rom 5)
As people of hope and disciples of holy love, let us share
signs of joy and peace with one another this day.

Response to the Word (Gen 18, Matt 10)
When trouble knocks,
God answers the door.
    When despair comes to call,
    Christ shows it the door.
When illness threaten to bring us low,
the Spirit lifts us up.
    Our faith resides in God,
    for whom all things are possible.

Thanksgiving and Communion

Offering Prayer (Gen 18, Rom 5, Matt 9)
Touch these gifts, O God,
    with your manifold blessings.

Touch our very lives,
    that we may be instruments of your hope.
May our gifts and our lives,
    bring your healing, love, and compassion
        to a world in need. Amen.

Sending Forth

Benediction (Gen 18, Rom 5)
Go now in peace, but be prepared to laugh with Sarah.
Go now in hope, and be ready for unexpected miracles.
Go now in love, for the one who loves us goes with us.

June 21, 2020

Third Sunday after Pentecost, Proper 7
B. J. Beu
Copyright © B. J. Beu

Color

Green

Scripture Readings

Genesis 21:8-21; Psalm 86:1-10, 16-17; Romans 6:1b-11;
Matthew 10:24-39

Theme Ideas

Happy reading these are not. In Genesis, jealous that
Hagar's son will one day inherit with her son Isaac, Sarah asks Abraham to cast mother and son out into the
desert. Despite his distress, Abraham does so, because
God says to listen to Sarah! As Ishmael lies dying of
thirst, God seems unmoved by Hagar's tears, and steps
in only to save mother and child upon hearing the boy's
cries. In Matthew, Jesus warns that he did not come to
bring peace, but a sword, and to set a son against his
father, and a daughter against her mother. Either God
is ethically challenged, or God's purposes are beyond
our simple delineations of right and wrong. In seeming

answer, the psalmist cries out in distress, pleading her case before God, who is unlike the other gods—because God hears our prayers and listens to the cries of our supplications. God's ways are not our ways, but there is help in the Lord and in no other.

Invitation and Gathering

Centering Words (Ps 86)

Great are the works of God's hands. Wondrous are the blessings of Christ's love. Holy are the works of God's Spirit.

Call to Worship (Gen 21, Ps 86)

When we have been cast aside
in the deserts of our lives,
> **you open our eyes to life-giving water**
> **that sustains us in our need.**

When our future seems lost
and others have taken our place of honor,
> **you restore our hope**
> **and promise us an inheritance of our own.**

Who is like you among the gods?
> **Who answers prayer in times of deepest need?**

We are here to worship you, O God,
> **for you alone can save us.**

Opening Prayer (Gen 21, Matt 10)

Eternal God, turn and be gracious to us,
> for the road is long and we are weary.

We feel beaten down by the trials of life
> and need your strength to sustain us.

Show us your favor,
    and offer us your blessing,
        that we may abide in faithfulness
           and not be put to shame.
Comfort us, O God,
    and revive our souls.
Grant us the endurance to take up our cross,
    and follow the difficult roads in life. Amen.

Proclamation and Response

Prayer of Confession (Matt 10:26 NRSV)

Holy One, your words cause us to tremble:
    "nothing is covered up that will not be uncovered,
        and nothing secret that will not be known."
There is much in our lives
    that we wish to hide from others, even ourselves.
We fear those who kill the body,
    while ignoring those who kill the soul.
Teach us once more, O God,
    that your Son came to bring us life—
        even if turned son against father,
           and daughter against mother.
Remind us of our higher calling,
    and the promises you offer
        of life in your realm
           which has no end. Amen.

Words of Assurance (Matt 10, Rom 6)

Those who seek to preserve their life will lose it,
    but those who lose their life for Christ's sake
    will find it.
Those who have died with Christ through baptism
    are united with him in his resurrection.

Response to the Word (Gen 21)

It is hard to hear difficult news, O God.
It is humbling to remember
that your ways are not our ways,
that we rarely know
what is truly good for us.
May the story of Sarah's inhumanity
move us to face our own.
May Abraham's refusal to stand up for his son
remind us of the need to protect and defend
the ones we love.
Help us discern your will, O God.
that we might know what is right
and pursue the paths that lead to life. Amen.

—*Or*—

Response to the Word (Ps 86)

We lift up our souls, O Lord, ~~for~~ your goodness heals our ills,
your forgiveness is sweeter than honey.
Your steadfast love strengthens all who call upon you.
Listen to our cries of supplication,
and the deepest calling of our hearts.
For you alone can hear us.
You alone can mend our hurts
and bind our wounds. Amen .

Prayer of Petition (Ps 86)

We come in our need, O God.
We come in our loneliness and want.
You alone know my suffering, our pain.
You alone know the depth of our grief.

138

Raise us from the grave of doubt and despair.
Raise us up from the death of superficiality.
You alone know our suffering and our pain.
You alone know the depth of our grief.

Thanksgiving and Communion

Offering Prayer (Ps 86)
Receive the gifts of our hands, O God,
that they may be signs of your love and grace
for a divided world.
Through our offerings,
help others follow the ways of life.
Fill the world with your mercy, Holy One,
that your faithful everywhere will honor you,
by sharing your kingdom
each and every day. Amen.

Sending Forth

Benediction (Gen 21)
Though we have been cast aside,
you restore our future.
Though others seek to banish us from sight,
you bless us with opportunities for new life.
Go with the blessings of the one who loves us fiercely.
We go to share God' love with the world.

June 28, 2020

Fourth Sunday after Pentecost, Proper 8
Michelle L. Torigian

Color

Green

Scripture Readings

Genesis 22:1-14; Psalm 13; Romans 6:12-23;
Matthew 10:40-42

Theme Ideas

The items, the relationships, and the emotions we cling
to define us. The lectionary texts provide a chance to
examine the items we hoard in our hearts that distract
us from our relationship with God. The divine request
to release all that we have to God is woven throughout
the Genesis and Matthew texts. Abraham is asked to
release Isaac. Jesus proclaims that our love of human
family must not supersede our love of the divine.
Attachments to human family can distract us from God's
call. Likewise, Romans reminds us that God's grace releases us from the sin and shame we amass when we
wander away. Becoming free from the weights of this
life, and placing our trust in the divine, allow us to focus
on God. Psalm 13 addresses what allows us to release: "I
trusted in your steadfast love" (v. 5 NRSV).

Invitation and Gathering

Centering Words (Gen 22, Matt 10, Rom 6)

Our hearts are weighed down by our attachments in this life. As we enter a time of worship, may we exhale our worries and inhale the Spirit of God that surrounds us. May we find here a space for release and reflection—a space to empty our souls and create a refuge for Sabbath rest.

Call to Worship (Ps 13, Rom 6)

How long, O Lord?
> **How long must we hold onto this pain?**

How long will the aches of our souls
have power over our hearts?
> **How long must we bear the weights of worry,**
> **of guilt, of sorrow?**

Move beyond the past that holds us captive.
> **We will move forward, despite the scars.**

May God's steadfast love heal our spirits.
> **May God's steadfast love**
> **help us discover the road to salvation.**

Let us sing with renewed voices.
> **Let us sing of divine generosity.**

Opening Prayer (Gen 22, Ps 13, Matt 10)

Holy One, in whom we bear our souls,
> we take comfort and courage in your presence.

Through your love and light,
> we are able to explore what it takes
> to place our trust entirely in you.

Help us lovingly put you before all else,
> as we journey the corridors of uncertainty,
> knowing that your steadfast love
> shepherds us on paths unknown. Amen.

Proclamation and Response

Prayer of Confession (Rom 6)

Spirit of Creation, whose steadfast love drapes the earth,
    our human limitations shroud us from you,
    prodding us to unhealthy tendencies.
We choose discordant noises,
instead of the melodious sounds of your call.
We would rather abide in the vapors of worry,
and the smog of self-interest,
    rather than breathe the refreshing mist
        of your grace.
May the toxic clouds that confine our spirits dissipate,
    and may we perceive the light of your grace. Amen.

Words of Assurance (Rom 6)

God releases creation from the haze of separation—
    the division separating us from God
    and our neighbors from ourselves.
In the spirit of God's freedom,
    let us delight in the refreshing winds of God's grace,
    renewing us all. Amen.

Passing the Peace of Christ (Rom 6)

Pain and hurt have no dominion over us when we share
this sanctuary with one another. Let us share a greeting
of peace and love with neighbors, enemies, strangers,
and friends alike.

Response to the Word (Matt 10, Ps 13, Rom 6, Gen 22)

What does taking up our cross look like in the world?
    **How does loving God more than our friends
    and family work?**

142

Let us find ways to authentically find our lives—
   risking what we need,
   learning how to love radically,
   and walking in the steps of Jesus.
As we pour out our self-interests,
let us drink the steadfast love of God.
   Let us absorb salvation and abiding grace.
   Amen.

Thanksgiving and Communion

Invitation to the Offering (Matt 10, Ps 13)

Trusting in the steadfast love of God requires us to invest our whole selves—from the depths of our souls, and with the entirety of our hearts. Now is the time to share what we have been given. This is the place to welcome the Spirit of Christ. With our whole selves, let us present what we have received from God, back to God.

Offering Prayer (Matt 10, Ps 13)

Through the teachings of Jesus,
   the steadfast love of God,
      and the empowering winds of the Spirit,
         we have been taught to share what we have,
            our time, talent, and treasure,
               with those in need.
As we serve our neighbors,
   we serve the Christ.
In gratitude for God's many gifts,
   we celebrate God's call to care for creation,
      and to boldly love the children of God. Amen.

Invitation to Communion
> Through the steadfast love of God,
> we come to this table.
>> **Through the steadfast love of Christ,**
>> **we share this meal.**
> Our hearts rejoice in the saving love of our creator.
>> **Our souls sing alleluia with the saving love**
>> **of our redeemer.**
> May the Spirit be with you.
>> **And also with you.**
> Share your hearts freely.
>> **We share them courageously with one another.**
> In this time and space we delight in our creator,
>> **we sing joyfully of God's care for us.**
> A table was shaped so beautifully
>> with round edges and smooth corners—
>> a table wide enough for the diversity
>> of the body of Christ,
>> a table able to stretch from pole to pole.
> As we savor this sacrament,
>> remembering the one who gave us this meal,
>> we recall that Christ abides with us, here and now.

Communion Prayer
> Holy One, send your Spirit to encircle this table
>> with your love.
> Bless all who are present, here and now,
>> and all who are present in our hearts. Amen.

Sending Forth

Benediction (Psalm 13, Matthew 10, Genesis 22, Romans 6)
> God's steadfast love is etched into our souls.
> May we carry it with us always.

Whether welcoming the stranger,
    whether risking all we have,
    whether facing the cross,
    whether wrestling with God's call,
    whether freeing ourselves from our past,
    God is our constant companion on this journey.
Amen!

July 5, 2020

Fifth Sunday after Pentecost, Proper 9
Mary Scifres
Copyright © Mary Scifres

Color

Green

Scripture Readings

Genesis 24:34-38, 42-49, 58-67; Psalm 45:10-17;
Romans 7:15-25a, Matthew 11:16-19, 25-30

Theme Ideas

Today's readings offer interesting treatments of the
yokes we encounter in life. Rebekah immediately accepts the yoke of marriage when she is approached by
the servant of her distant relative Isaac. Her family then
sends her on this new venture with prayers and blessings for a fruitful and joy-filled life. Paul laments his resistance to the yoke of obedience to the law, but thanks
Christ for making possible the fruitful and joy-filled
life of following God—a life for which Paul yearns. In
Matthew, Jesus warns that the children of "this generation" (11:16) are a rebellious and resistant lot, dancing
to their own beat rather than to the rhythm of following

God. Yet this passage concludes with a promise that the yoke of Christ will be easy and renewing, rather than burdensome. Life does indeed bring yokes of various shapes and sizes—some we choose for ourselves, and some others choose for us. The mystery of life's yokes run through each of these readings, and challenge us to reflect on what it means to follow God, and what yokes might nourish or hinder that journey.

Invitation and Gathering

Centering Words (Matt 11:28)
"Come to me...and I will give you rest," Jesus promises. Where do we go, and to whom do we turn, to discover the truth of these words?

Call to Worship (Matt 11)
The music is playing, and God is calling.
We have come to sing and dance with God.
The prayers are flowing, and Spirit is moving.
Breathe on us, breath of God.
Christ promises rest and renewal, when we come to him.
We are here, trusting this sacred promise.

Opening Prayer (Matt 11)
Creator God, you have created us to walk with you.
Help us walk with you in this time of worship,
    that we may be strengthened to walk with you
        all the days of our lives.
As we come to you this day,
    bless us with your grace and your rest,
        that we may find renewal
            and the strength to serve
                with confidence and joy. Amen.

Proclamation and Response

Call to Confession (Matt 11)

Come to Christ with the confidence of children, for Christ will carry our burdens, renew our souls, and give us rest, through his mercy and grace.

Prayer of Confession (Matt 11)

Prophetic One, you call us to new places and new ways.
You challenge us to dance new steps
    and to sing new songs.
We yearn to follow you with confidence and joy,
    but our resistance is often stronger
        than our willingness.
At times, our steps falter.
At moments, we can't even hear your voice,
    let alone recognize your song in our hearts.
Strengthen us with your mercy.
Renew us with your grace.
Sing to us with your compassion.
Connect us with the yoke of unconditional love,
    that we may follow joyously, dance confidently,
        and sing praise and love with every act
           and with every word of our lives.
In your holy name, we pray. Amen.

Words of Assurance (Matt 11)

Rejoice and give thanks.
With grace, Christ is already carrying our burdens
    to renew our souls.
With mercy, Christ is already shouldering our load
    to strengthen our lives.

Passing the Peace of Christ (Matt 11)
Let us share the joy, the freedom, and the rest we find in God's love, as we greet one another in the grace and peace of Christ.

Introduction to the Word (Matt 11)
Scripture is one of God's songs of love to us. Let us listen for the message of love this day.

Response to the Word (Matt 11)
In Christ, we are invited to lay our burdens down and to accept the rest and renewal that God gives. Let us take a moment in silent reflection, as we reflect on how to accept this invitation and discover new joy on our journeys of faith.

Thanksgiving and Communion

Invitation to the Offering (Matt 11)
Come to Christ and offer your gifts, not as a burden, but as an opportunity to give rest and renewal to those who yearn to know God's love.

Offering Prayer (Matt 11)
Receive these gifts we now bring, God of gifts,
    and bless them to be gifts for your world.
Through our giving, renew others,
    that they too may know the comfort and rest
        of living in the arms of your compassion
        and your love. Amen.

Invitation to Communion (Matt 11)

Come to the table of love.

At this table, we will find strength for our journeys
and rest for our souls.

Sending Forth

Benediction (Matt 11)

Go forth, as people renewed by the love of God.

Go forth, to renew others with this very love.

July 12, 2020

Sixth Sunday after Pentecost, Proper 10
B. J. Beu

Color

Green

Scripture Readings

Genesis 25:19-34; Psalm 119:105-112; Romans 8:1-11; Matthew 13:1-9, 18-23

Theme Ideas

God is the sower; we are the seed. Matthew's parable of the Sower mirrors the reality of our world. The word of God simply does not seem to take root in some people; or if it does, it quickly burns out. And despite God's life-giving precepts and teachings, some people choose to follow their baser instincts, which Paul calls living "according to the flesh" (Rom 8:5 NRSV). In the church, we believe that the soil of our lives can change. The cares of the world sometimes choke the word that people hear, but it need not be so forever. Yet, it always seems to be a struggle—a struggle reflected in Genesis' account of Rebekah's children struggling within her.

Two parents struggle to love their children, yet each has a favorite. Two brothers struggle to find their place in God's world as they answer God's call. Today's scriptures reflect these struggles, even as they offer a lamp to our feet and a light for our journey.

Invitation and Gathering

Centering Words (Matt 13)
Ask the Sower to cast you onto good, fertile soil, that you may bear the fruit of faith and love.

Call to Worship (Matt 13)
You are the Sower, O God, we are the seed.
God's word is being sown in our lives this day
with the promise of new growth.
You are the Lover, O God, we are the beloved.
God's love blossoms in our lives
with a beauty greater than the lilies of the field.
You are the Healer, O God, we are the healed.
God's healing flows through our lives
with every beat of our heart.
You are the Potter, O God, we are the clay.
God's hand fashions us to shine
with the glory of Christ's light.
Come! Let us worship the one
who sows us in fields of love.

—Or—

Call to Worship (Matt 13)
We are like seeds on the wind,
set free by the Sower.

**The hand of God saves us
from the rocky pathways
and the thorny ground.**
In Christ, we find good soil.
The Holy Spirit nourishes us as we grow.
Come! Let us worship the Sower,
who plants us in the fields of life.

Opening Prayer (Matt 13)
Great Sower, cast us like seeds
upon the winds of your mercy,
that we may grow in fertile ground.
Keep our lives from stony pathways,
where the heat of life's cares and strife
strip our strength and vitality.
Protect us from thorny gullies,
where the snares of life's worries and fears
block the sunshine of your Spirit.
Land us safely in rich soil, Master Gardener,
and bless us with the kiss of gentle rain,
that our faith may increase
and our joy may be complete. Amen.

Proclamation and Response

Prayer of Yearning (Matt 13, Rom 8, Ps 119)
Caretaker of our souls, we yearn to resist the allures
of status and prestige,
for we often pierce ourselves with wounds
of our own making.
We long to bloom where we are planted,
that righteousness and peace
might flower in our lives.

Free us of the fear of appearing foolish before others,
>   as we seek new growth in your Spirit.
Nurture us with your grace and mercy,
>   that we might blossom and bloom
>   as followers of Christ. Amen.

Words of Assurance (Rom 8, Matt 13)

Those who abide in the Spirit are set free.
Those who reside in Christ find no condemnation.
Rejoice that we have been planted in the fertile ground
>   of God's love and mercy.

Passing the Peace of Christ (Matt 13)

The Sower has planted us in the fertile ground of this church. Let us express our gratitude for the love that grows within our fellowship by offering one another signs of Christ's peace.

Introduction to the Word

Do not give up on us, O God,
>   for we are here to follow your precepts
>   and return to your ways.
Speak to us again of your ways of life and death,
>   that we may grow strong in our faith
>   and bear the fruit of eternal life. Amen.

Response to the Word (Ps 119)

Your word is a lamp to our feet, O God.
>   **Your instructions are a light to our path.**
Your decrees are a living heritage.
>   **Your teachings are a blessing in times of trial.**
Hold our hands and guide us, Holy One.
>   **Help us abide in your ways.**

Call to Prayer (Ps 119)

Though the wicked may lay snares for us,
   in God we dwell secure.
Though the shadows of life may obscure our path,
   God is a lamp to our feet
   and a light to our path.
Come, let us offer our prayers and petitions
   to the one who brings joy to our hearts
   and healing to our wounds.
Let us pray together.

Thanksgiving and Communion

Invitation to the Offering (Matt 13)

Like a field ready for harvest,
   our lives bear the marks
      of God's love and care.
May we, who bear the fruit of God's labor,
   rejoice as people who have been blessed
   with a bounty not of our making.
With love and thanksgiving,
   let us bring our tithes and offerings
   to those in need.

Offering Prayer (Matt 13)

Master Gardener, as you have sown our lives
   in a rich and fertile soil,
      may we bear much fruit through our giving.
With these offerings,
   may your realm be brought to earth,
      as we plant seeds of hope in the fields of life.
Bless our gifts and our ministry,
   that the world may reap a harvest
      of generosity and love. Amen.

Sending Forth

Benediction (Ps 119, Matt 13)

God's word is a lamp to our feet.
Christ's teachings are a light to our path.
May God's word take root in our lives.
**May Christ's love nourish us like sunshine
and spring rain.**
God's word is a lamp to our feet.
Christ's teachings are a light to our path.

July 19, 2020

Seventh Sunday after Pentecost, Proper 11
Mary Scifres
Copyright © Mary Scifres

Color

Green

Scripture Readings

Genesis 28:10-19a; Psalm 139:1-12, 23-24;
Romans 8:12-25; Matthew 13:24-30, 36-43

Theme Ideas

The best is yet to come, or so it would seem from today's readings. As his father and grandfather before
him, Jacob receives God's promise that he will one day
be blessed to bless others. Paul calls the Romans to wait
with patience for the fulfillment of God's promised
adoption—an adoption that will usher in the new creation where we will live as God's children. In Matthew,
Jesus warns that as we await God's realm to come to fru-
ition, we will live side by side, wheat and weed, even as
we are called to remain fruitful, healthy fields of grain.
The best is clearly not here yet, and so we wait—with
patience, steadfast faithfulness, perseverance, and hope.

Invitation and Gathering

Centering Words (Rom 8)

While we are waiting, God is waiting with us. God's promises are both now and yet to come. Wait and see.

Call to Worship (Rom 8, Matt 13)

We wait with hope,
> **for God's promises are sure.**

We wait with patience,
> **for God's time is a mystery.**

Come and worship.
> **We will wait upon the Lord together.**

Opening Prayer (Gen 28, Rom 8)

Holy God of mystery and miracles,
> reveal your presence to us,
> > as we gather in worship.

Send your Holy Spirit to descend upon us,
> as angels once descended to Jacob.

Raise our thoughts,
> that we may reflect on your promises
> > and trust with hope
> > > in promises yet to come.

In your holy name, we pray. Amen

Proclamation and Response

Prayer of Confession (Matt 13, Rom 8)

Patient, loving God,
> when we are groaning and griping,
> > comfort us and forgive our shortcomings.

When we are doubting and afraid,
> comfort us and reveal your promises to us.

Help us trust with hope,
>and wait with patience,
>>even as you patiently love us
>>>with your mercy and your grace.
In your loving name, we pray. Amen.

Words of Assurance (Rom 8)

We have this hope: God's promises are sure,
>and Christ's mercy is ours.
All is well. All will be well.

Passing the Peace of Christ (Rom 8)

As God's beloved children, let us share signs of love and peace with our sisters and brothers in Christ.

Introduction to the Word (Gen 28)

Here in the house of God, let us open our minds, as we listen for the word of God.

Response to the Word (Rom 8, Matt 13)

Wheat or weeds, we are planted in God's garden.
>**We are waiting and growing in God.**
Children of hope, we are welcomed in God's family.
>**We are waiting and loving with God.**

Thanksgiving and Communion

Offering Prayer (Gen 28, Rom 8)

God of ancient times and future hope,
>we bring these gifts to bless your world with hope.
Please bless these gifts,
>that they may be a blessing to others.
And bless us with patience and faith,
>that we may bring hope to a hurting world. Amen.

Sending Forth

Benediction (Rom 8)

> May patience pave our path.
> May hope comfort our world.
> And may love guide our lives.
> Go with patience, hope, and love.

July 26, 2020

Eighth Sunday after Pentecost, Proper 12
Karin Ellis

Color

Green

Scripture Readings

Genesis 29:15-28; Psalm 105:1-11, 45b; Romans 8:26-39; Matthew 13:31-33, 44-52

Theme Ideas

Today's lessons speak about the family of God. Genesis recounts the story of the beginnings of God's family with Laban and Jacob, while the psalmist remembers this story with praise and thanksgiving. In his letter to the Romans, Paul reminds the early church family that nothing can separate us from God because we have Christ Jesus, the one who died for us and intercedes for us. And Matthew identifies how the family of God should live, seeking out the kingdom and helping to make it a reality here on earth. From the very beginning, God has always been with us as we grow to be the family of Christ.

Invitation and Gathering

Centering Words (Ps 105)

No matter what happened yesterday, now is the time to call upon God, to lay our lives before our creator, and to proclaim God's wonderful deeds to one another. Now is the time to worship.

Call to Worship (Ps 105)

Praise the Lord!
We gather to sing praises to God.
Praise the Lord!
**We gather to give thanks
for all God has done in our lives.**
Praise the Lord!
**We gather to worship our creator, redeemer,
and sustainer.**

Opening Prayer (Gen 29, Rom 8)

Holy One, we come before you
with sighs too deep for words.
We come with hearts overwhelmed—
by the world, by personal relationships,
and by inward struggles.
We come to praise your name
and to be reassured of your unending grace.
In this time and place,
open our hearts to your presence.
Open our ears to hear your word proclaimed.
Open our hands to serve you and the world.
May our lives reflect Christ,
who walks with us and gives us life.
In the name of Christ, we pray. Amen.

Proclamation and Response

Prayer of Confession (Rom 8)

Loving God, you search our hearts
to see all the good,
all the challenges,
and all the obstacles in our lives.
You remember the times
we have turned away from you—
the times we have forgotten
we are your beloved children.
Forgive us when we do not act
as your faithful followers.
Remind us we are a part of your family.
May your Son, Jesus Christ,
intercede in our lives
to bring us grace and healing.
Help us be your servants
and share your story with the world.
In your precious name, we pray. Amen.

Words of Assurance (Rom 8)

Beloved children of God,
nothing in this life can separate us
from the love of God in Christ Jesus our Lord.
Receive the forgiveness of God,
and go forth to be the loving community of faith.
Amen.

Passing the Peace of Christ (Rom 8)

The peace of Christ be with you.
And also with you.
Knowing the Spirit intercedes for us and is with us

always, I invite you to turn and greet one another in the
Spirit of Christ.

Prayer of Preparation (Rom 8)

Holy One, fill our hearts with your Spirit.
Open our ears to hear your word proclaimed.
Remind us that you are always with us,
    guiding us to be your faithful disciples. Amen.

Response to the Word (Gen 29, Matt 13)

We give thanks, O God, for the word proclaimed,
    the music shared, and the prayers spoken.
And now, as kingdom people,
    may your Holy Spirit empower us to live together
        as your family. Amen.

Thanksgiving and Communion

Invitation to the Offering (Matt 13)

Christ reminds us that our treasures, our gifts from God,
are most beneficial when they are used for the kingdom
of God. May this be the time when we bring forth our
gifts to be blessed by God.

Offering Prayer (Rom 8, Matt 13)

Almighty God, there are treasures all around us—
    family, friends, your abiding presence,
    and the love of Christ Jesus.
Bless these gifts we return to you now.
Bless them,
    that others might come to know
        the true treasures of your love and grace.
In your holy name, we pray. Amen.

Sending Forth

Benediction (Gen 29, Ps 105, Rom 8, Matt 13)
Go forth knowing that you are part of God's family.
Go forth proclaiming the praises of God.
Go forth in the assurance that Christ is always with us.
Go forth to bring the kingdom of God wherever you are.

August 2, 2020

Ninth Sunday after Pentecost, Proper 13
Mary Scifres
Copyright © Mary Scifres

Color

Green

Scripture Readings

Genesis 32:22-31; Psalm 17:1-7, 15; Romans 9:1-5;
Matthew 11, 14:13-21

Theme Ideas

Night-time miracles occur in today's reading from Genesis and Matthew. In Matthew's feeding of the five thousand, it is evening, and the disciples are ready to rest. As Jacob prepares to meet his brother Esau, it is nightfall, and he and his family are ready to rest. In both cases, this rest is interrupted by miraculous encounters of divine power. Jacob wrestles with an angel and receives a blessing. The disciples debate with Jesus about sending the crowds away to find their own food, and instead witness a miraculous feast from some loaves of bread and a couple of fish. Even in our darkest hours and times of greatest fatigue, God is with us, offering miraculous opportunities for blessing and ministry.

Invitation and Gathering

Centering Words (Gen 32, Matt 14)

In our darkest hours, God's light continues to shine. In our weariest moments, God's strength is enough. In our times of greatest isolation, God's presence is always near.

Call to Worship (Gen 32, Matt 14, Matt 11)

Come, all who are weary.
Christ strengthens us with love and grace.
In this strength, we can do all things.
We are here, ready to receive God's blessings.

Opening Prayer (Matt 14)

Mighty God, pour out your power and strength on us.
Grant us the nourishment we need to receive your word.
May your presence fill our lives and carry us forth,
preparing us to be your people
and equipping us to do your work in the world.
In your holy name, we pray. Amen

Proclamation and Response

Prayer of Yearning (Gen 32, Matt 14, Rom 9)

Come to us, Holy One,
even in our times of resistance.
Work within and through us,
even when we wrestle with doubt and despair.
Enlighten and guide us,
even in our darkest hours.
Bless us and call us by name,
even when we reject your presence.

Hold us and love us,
    even when we try to run away.
When we feel beat down by the world,
    and are weary with fatigue and sorrow,
        nourish us with your mercy and your grace.
Fill us with your love,
    that we may go forth with confidence and faith.
In your mighty name, we pray. Amen.

Words of Assurance (Gen 32, Matt 14)

God's strength is enough.
Christ's forgiveness is sure.
Through God's strength and Christ's grace,
    we are blessed, loved, and made whole.

Introduction to the Word (Gen 32, Matt 14)

Pay attention, for in God's word, we may discover an
unexpected blessing; we may find nourishment for our
souls.

Thanksgiving and Communion

Invitation to the Offering (Matt 14)

Whatever our gifts—a loaf of bread, a tiny coin, a mighty
blessing, or an amazing talent—each gift matters. Whatever our gifts, our gifts become miracles when we share
them with God and with God's people.

Offering Prayer (Gen 32, Matt 14)

Holy Spirit, as you blessed Jacob long ago,
    bless us now.
As you blessed bread and fish on a Galilean shore,
    bless and transform these gifts
        into abundant blessings for those is need;

bless and guide our ministries
    into avenues for your mercy and grace.
In your blessed name, we pray. Amen.

Invitation to Communion (Matt 14)

As Jesus welcomed the thousands to share in a feast created from a few loaves and some fish, Christ welcomes
us now to this abundant feast of holy communion,
where we are fed with God's grace and love.

The Great Thanksgiving (Gen 32, Matt 14)

The Lord be with you.
    And also with you.
Lift up your hearts.
    We lift them up to the Lord.
Let us give thanks to the Lord, our God.
    It is right to give our thanks and praise.

It is right, and a good and joyful thing,
    always and everywhere to give thanks to you,
    almighty God, creator of heaven and earth.
You formed us in your image,
    breathing into us the breath of life.
You wrestled with our ancestors in the desert,
    came to us in night times of weariness,
    confusion and doubt,
    and guided us as a pillar of light
    and a blessing of love
When our faith faltered and we rejected your guidance,
    you spoke to us of love and compassion,
    through the law and the prophets.
Always, your love remained steadfast.

Always, you deliver us from death and despair,
  and call us to return and follow you.

And so, with your people on earth,
  and all the company of heaven,
  we praise your name
  and join their unending hymn, saying:
  Holy, holy, holy Lord, God of power and might,
    Heaven and earth are full of your glory.
  Hosanna in the highest! Blessed is the one
    who comes in the name of the Lord.
  Hosanna in the highest!

Holy are you, and blessed is your beloved child,
  Christ Jesus, who blessed and broke bread
  for thousands on a shore of Galilee.
He healed the sick and taught your love,
  as he walked up on this earth.
In Christ's great love, you gave birth to your Church,
  delivered us from the weary burden of sin,
  and freed us to receive your blessing and love,
  both now and into eternity.

On his last night, before meeting death, at a last supper,
  Jesus blessed and broke bread one last time,
  feeding his disciples with these words:
  "Take, eat; this is my body, which is given for you."
After supper, he took the cup, giving thanks yet again,
  and gave it to his disciples, saying,
  "Drink from this, all of you; this is my life,
  which is poured out for you and for many
  for the forgiveness of sins. As often as you drink it,
  do so in remembrance of me."

And so, in remembrance of these,
> your miraculous acts in Christ Jesus,
> we offer ourselves in praise and thanksgiving,
> as a holy and living sacrifice,
> in union with Christ's offering for us,
> as we proclaim the mystery of faith.
> **Christ has died.**
> **Christ is risen.**
> **Christ will come again.**

Communion Prayer (Gen 32, Matt 14)

Pour out your Holy Spirit on us,
> that we might know your blessing
>> and receive your grace.

Pour out your Holy Spirit
> on these gifts of bread and wine.

May they nourish us as bread that never ends
> and as living water that always satisfies.

By your Spirit, make us one with Christ,
> one with each other,
>> and one in ministry to the world,
>>> until Christ comes again in final victory,
>>>> and we feast at the heavenly banquet.

Through Jesus Christ and the Holy Spirit,
> all honor and glory is yours, almighty God,
>> now and forevermore. Amen.

Giving the Bread and Cup

(The bread and wine are given to the people, with these or other words of blessing.)
The bread of life, to feed your soul.
The living water, to nourish your life.

Sending Forth

Benediction (Gen 32)

As we have received light,
we go now to bring light to the world.
As we have received God's blessings,
we go now to be blessings to others.

August 9, 2020

Tenth Sunday after Pentecost, Proper 14

B. J. Beu

Color

Green

Scripture Readings

Genesis 37:1-4, 12-28; Psalm 105:1-6, 16-22, 45b;
Romans 10:5-15; Matthew 14:22-33

Theme Ideas

Even in the midst of our failings, God can turn human
weakness into acts of deliverance. Genesis 37 begins
the story of Joseph's sale into slavery by his brothers.
Psalm 105 proclaims that God used this act of human
betrayal to deliver all the lands from the effects of famine. Paul proclaims that all who profess Christ with
their lips and believe in him with their whole heart
will be saved. Matthew 14 recalls the story of Peter's
fear and doubt as he walks on the water toward Jesus.
Jesus rescues Peter from the sea and admonishes him
for his doubts.

Invitation and Gathering

Centering Words (Gen 37)

God can turn even our worst moments into possibilities for good. God can transform even our worst experiences into opportunities for grace.

Call to Worship (Gen 37, Ps 105, Rom 10)

Give thanks to the Lord.
Call on God's holy name.
    Rejoice in the Lord.
    God fills our hearts with joy.
Give thanks to the Lord.
Proclaim God's mighty works.
    Rejoice in the Lord.
    God's miracles are a wonder to behold.
Give thanks to the Lord.
Trust in God's salvation.
    Rejoice in the Lord.
    God turns even our failings into glory.

—Or—

Call to Worship (Matt 14)

Jesus walks to us over the water.
    "Call to us, Lord. We long to be with you."
Jesus calls to us, "Come! Do not be afraid."
    "Save us, Lord, we're sinking!"
Jesus saves us from our fears.
God delivers us from the storm.
    Thanks be to God!

Opening Prayer (Gen 37, Ps 105, Rom 10:15 NRSV, Matt 14)

Eternal God, you visit us in dreams,
    offering us glimpses of new possibilities.

Rescue us from life's storms,
    and lift us from the raging waters.
Be with us now, as we call on your name.
Reveal your purposes for our world,
    that we may be of use and service.
Bless us with the courage to spread your word,
    that it may be said of us:
    "How beautiful are the feet
      of those who bring good news!"

Proclamation and Response

Prayer of Confession (Gen 37, Matt 14)
God of infinite possibilities,
    we are like a boat that is beaten by the storm:
      without your aid we are powerless
        to get where we are going;
    we are like disciples who sit in fear for their lives:
      without your presence we are trapped
        within the prison of our feelings
        of helplessness;
    we are like those lost in wonder and disbelief:
      without your assurance we quickly drown
        in our hopeless and despair.
Grant us the courage of Peter
    to believe that through your power
      anything is possible.
Give us the confidence of Joseph
    to live as dreamers,
      even when the world turns against us,
      that we may always be found faithful. Amen.

Assurance of Pardon (Rom 10:11, 13 NRSV)

Christ's love is greater than our deepest failings.
"The scripture says, 'No one who believes in him
will be put to shame.' ...
For, 'Everyone who calls on the name of the Lord
will be saved.'"

Response to the Word (Rom 10:14-15 NRSV)

We live in a world full of people who know more of Santa
Clauses and Easter Bunnies than they do of mangers and
empty tombs. We live among neighbors who hunger for
spiritual truth but do not know where it may be found.
Paul's question is as true today as it was two thousand
years ago: "How are they to believe in one of whom they
have never heard? And how are they to hear without
someone to proclaim him? ... As it is written, 'How beautiful are the feet of those who bring good news!'"

Thanksgiving and Communion

Offering Prayer (Gen 37, Ps 105)

Loving God, your mercies know no bounds.
Though his own brothers threw him into a pit
and sold him into slavery,
Joseph remained faithful.
Though his feet were bound with chains
and his neck with a collar of iron,
Joseph placed his fate in your hands.
May our lives reflect this same devotion
in all our endeavors.
And may our offering be a sign
of our faithfulness to you, O God,
our savior and deliverer. Amen.

Sending Forth

Benediction (Ps 105, Matt 14)

God blesses us with strength for the journey.
> **Our hearts sing God's praises.**

Christ lifts us up from the raging waters of life.
> **Our spirits rejoice in our salvation.**

The Spirit guides us with dreams full of hope
and promise.
> **Our lives rest secure in the One who is faithful.**

Thanks be to God!

August 16, 2020

Eleventh Sunday after Pentecost, Proper 15
B. J. Beu
Copyright © B. J. Beu

Color

Green

Scripture Readings

Genesis 22, 45:1-15; Psalm 133; Romans 6, 11:1-2a, 29-32;
Matthew 15:(10-20) 21-28

Theme Ideas

What unites us is far greater than what divides us. Joseph forgives his brothers for selling him into slavery, for God used this terrible act to save Israelites and Egyptians alike from famine. The psalmist celebrates when kindred live together in unity. Paul asks rhetorically if God has rejected the Hebrew people by offering salvation to the Gentiles, and answers no. Jesus initially refuses to help a Canaanite woman's daughter until she presses her case. Then Jesus joyfully heals the daughter, marveling at the mother's faith. We are all bound together in the unconditional love of God.

Invitation and Gathering

Centering Words

> When all seems to be lost, God is most near to us.

Call to Worship (Gen 45, Ps 133, Rom 11, Matt 15)

When hatred and division separate us,
> **God's love binds us together.**

When quarrels estrange us from one another,
> **Christ's light shows us the way to reconciliation.**

When we feel excluded and left out,
> **The Spirit's peace eases our pain.**

When all hope of fellowship seems lost,
> **God's grace restores our hope.**

Come! Let us worship God, who makes us one.

Opening Prayer (Gen 45, Ps 133, Rom 11, Matt 15)

Eternal God, part the veil that blinds us
> to our unity as your beloved children.

When those we love hurt and betray us,
> help us let go of our pain
>> and find the balm of forgiveness.

When we feel abandoned by those we trust,
> help us seek your peace and reconciliation.

When our hearts are pierced with anguish,
> help us find those who will bring us solace,
>> through your loving Spirit. Amen.

Proclamation and Response

Prayer of Yearning (Gen 45, Ps 133, Matt 15)

Merciful God, we yearn to be like the Joseph
> who wept with forgiveness
>> on the necks of those who sold him into slavery.

But we fear that our anger and resentment
would lead us to take retribution
on those who have wronged us.
We long to see in the Canaanite woman
a child of God worthy of mercy and compassion.
But we fear that our deep-seated prejudices
might lead us to dismiss her out of hand,
as Jesus's disciples did before us.
We want to open our hearts, O God,
to those who are different from ourselves.
But we fear to expect too much of ourselves.
Help us know the joy of living in peace and harmony,
even with those we would rather live without.

Assurance of Pardon (Rom 11)

The gifts and the calling of God are irrevocable.
Rejoice in the knowledge of God's saving love.

Response to the Word (Gen 45, Ps 133, Rom 11, Matt 15)

Even in the midst of apparent tragedy,
God's love gathers up the fragments of our lives.
**Even in the midst of apparent rejection,
God's faithfulness rescues us from despair.**
Even when we feel abandoned and alone,
God calls us to find strength for the journey.
**Even in the midst of strife,
God calls us to look beyond our differences
and live together in unity.**

Thanksgiving and Communion

Offering Prayer (Gen 22)

Bountiful God, when famine threatened the world,
you blessed Joseph with dreams
that saved children of every nation.

Faithful One, when hunger threatens our world,
    you bless us with dreams
        that we can save the children of our day.
Bless this offering,
    that your dreams for a world without want
        may bless the lives of your children.
Accept these gifts,
    as tokens of our dreams and our commitment
        to make all people one
           in your holy name. Amen.

Sending Forth

Benediction (Gen 22, Rom 6)
The God of dreams has brought us together.
    The God of dreams sends us forth
    to love one another well.
The God of love has knit us together in unity.
    The God of love sends us forth
    to heal our divisions.
The God of hope sends us forth together.
    The God of peace sends us forth
    to bring the world home.

August 23, 2020

Twelfth Sunday after Pentecost, Proper 16
Rebecca Gaudino

Color

Green

Scripture Readings

Exodus 1:8–2:10; Psalm 124; Romans 12:1-8;
Matthew 16:13-20

Theme Ideas

Caesarea Philippi was one of the capitals of Philip the
Tetrarch, son of Herod the Great, who built a splendid
temple in this very area to the "son of god," Caesar Au-
gustus. For several decades, Philip minted coins with
this temple depicted on one side and Caesar's face on
the other. Against this backdrop of human power, we
hear Peter's declaration of faith—"You are the Messiah,
the Son of the living God" (Matt 16:16 NRSV)—counter-
manding human rulers who serve deathly powers-that-
be (see Exod 1–2). By choosing someone like Peter to be
the foundation of the church, Jesus indicates the radically different kingdom he is inaugurating in the world.
God strengthens, saves, and transforms all members of

God's church—weary and energized, weak and strong,
fallen and true—so that "the gates of the underworld"
(Matt 16:18) will not prevail in our community and in
this world.

Invitation and Gathering

Centering Words (Ps 124, Matt 16, Rom 12)
Seek the living God, who rescues and saves us in times
of trial. Seek the living God, who renews, transforms,
and strengthens us in our hour of need.

Call to Worship (Exod 1–2, Ps 124, Matt 16, Rom 12)
We step off the streets, away from places of work,
shopping malls, billboards, and news broadcasts,
to stand before the living God.
Our help is in the name of the living God,
maker of heaven and earth.
We turn away from the world and the patterns of power
that too often hurt, trap, and swallow us up.
We stand before our helper, the God of mercy,
who rescues and renews us.
We come to this sanctuary seeking the living God,
maker of heaven and earth.
We present ourselves to the living God,
who is compassionate and merciful,
as a living and pleasing sacrifice.

Opening Prayer (Exod 1–2, Ps 124, Matt 16, Rom 12)
Maker of heaven and earth,
we come from different places
with our own place on the journey.
Some of us have succeeded and found favor.

Some of us have failed and seek reassurance.
Some of us feel trapped and helpless.
Some of us have escaped peril and feel great relief.
But no matter what our experience has been,
  we come here today to meet you in worship.
Remind us of your power and mercy.
Replenish our courage and vision.
Renew our identity as your people.
Reinvigorate our holy work in this world,
    for our help is in your name alone, Holy God,
      maker of heaven and earth. Amen.

Proclamation and Response

Prayer of Confession (Exod 1–2, Ps 124, Rom 12)
God of mercy and grace,
  it is hard to hold onto hope.
We see people handed over
  as food for the enemies' teeth,
    or as prey for the hunters' traps.
Sometimes we are the food and the prey.
Sometimes we are the enemy and the hunter.
Sometimes we are merely bystanders,
  too afraid or powerless to act as we should.
Forgive us, O God, when we accept things as they are.
Maker of heaven and earth, giver of hope,
  savior of the distressed,
    fill our imaginations and our hearts
      with your splendid vision for our world.
Transform and renew our minds,
  that we may discern what is good and pleasing to
    you in this world you love so deeply. Amen.

Words of Assurance (Matt 16, Rom 12)

Jesus promised that the gates of the underworld
would not be able to stand against the Church.
Each of us is part of this Church, this body of Christ.
Each of us has unique gifts and our own unique calling.
Know that through God's mercies, you are forgiven.
Know that God will bless you with new imaginings,
new thoughts, new hopes, and new courage,
that we too may stand *in your reign*,
against the gates of the underworld.

Passing the Peace of Christ (Matt 16, Rom 12)

We are one body in Christ, and we belong to one another in this family, the Church. Let us welcome one
another to our mutual home as we share the peace of
Christ.

Prayer of Preparation (Matt 16, Rom 12)

Holy and living God, you promise that our minds,
so easily molded in the ways of our world,
can be transformed in your grace,
and that our lives may be renewed
in this transformation.
Open our minds, imaginations, hearts, and wills,
that we may be made new
as beloved members of your Church. Amen.

Response to the Word (Matt 16, Rom 12)

Living God, with your power and vision,
we can prevail against the powers of death
and the forces of destruction;
we can escape the raging waters
and survive the damaging storms.
Lift us up from our weariness and hopelessness,
and save us from the temptation to conform
to the powers-that-be.

By your powerful and life-giving name,
    renew our minds and our lives,
        that we may stand against
            the gates of the underworld. Amen.

Thanksgiving and Communion

Invitation to the Offering (Rom 12)

Paul writes that we belong to one another, and are to serve one another with our gifts. This beautiful vision moves beyond the Church through the one who draws the world together in love. We all belong to one another and depend upon one another. So let us give of our presence and vision, our resources and efforts, for the saving of our world.

Offering Prayer (Exod 1–2, Ps 124, Matt 16, Rom 12)

O God, maker of heaven and earth,
    you are our help in the midst of need and danger.
Bless our gifts this day,
    that they may find their way
        to those who feel hopeless and without resource.
May our gifts be a sign of your hope and love,
    and may the people we help
        find their way to safety. Amen.

Sending Forth

Benediction (Exod 1–2, Ps 124, Matt 16, Rom 12)

No matter how the world has treated us,
whether we are powerful or powerless,
God renews our vision and energy,

calling us to works of transformation
by reflecting God's love and justice.
With God's power, we will stand against
the powers of destruction in our world.
With God's wisdom, let us resist the seductive forces
that lead us to shut down and give in.
With God's eye on the powerless,
we will cry out on behalf of those caught
in the teeth of their enemies.
With God's mercy, let us pull to safety
those caught in the raging waters.
With God's justice, we will stand with those
who are enslaved and beaten down.
For it is none other than Jesus, the Messiah,
Son of the Living God, who has built the Church,
and the gates of the underworld will never conquer God
and God's Church.
Amen and amen.

August 30, 2020

Thirteenth Sunday after Pentecost, Proper 17
Mary Scifres
Copyright © Mary Scifres

Color

Green

Scripture Readings

Exodus 3:1-15; Psalm 105:1-6, 23-26, 45c; Romans 12:9-21; Matthew 16:21-28

Theme Ideas

The holiness of the divine dominates the readings from Exodus and Matthew. As long as Peter focuses on the human path, he cannot understand Jesus's path forward. It is only in seeing Jesus's path as something godly and holy that the disciples are able to travel the path with Jesus toward the cross. Similarly, Moses encounters the burning bush to prepare him to receive the holy presence of God. Yet in the midst of these holy encounters, there is also a murky shadow of the cruel path that lies ahead for both of these important leaders. And in the midst of this shadow, there is the almost jarring invitation in Ephesians to overcome evil with good—for

Exodus reveals a God who will not only harden Pharaoh's heart, but will even visit death upon Pharaoh's people in order to secure the freedom of the Hebrew people. This holiness theme is complicated indeed!

Invitation and Gathering

Centering Words (Rom 12)

Let love guide your path, for love is the holiest path of all.

Call to Worship (Exod 3, Rom 12)

Holy, holy, holy.

Holy God is here.

Holy, holy, holy.

Love has called us here.

Holy, holy, holy.

We gather to worship our holy God.

Opening Prayer (Exod 3, Matt 16)

Holy God, we come this day,

into this sacred moment and this sacred space,

aware that your holiness is always around us.

As Moses before us,

when we turn aside from our daily tasks,

and we listen for your holy voice,

speak to us in holy mystery.

Surround us with your wondrous love,

that we might be wise enough

to understand your call

and be brave enough

to follow your path. Amen.

Proclamation and Response

Prayer of Confession (Exod 3, Rom 12, Matt 16)
In the midst of your holy presence, O God,
　　we encounter a mystery
　　　　deeper than the foundations of the earth.
You are who you are,
　　sacred and indefinable.
Forgive us when we try to put you in a box,
　　or frame you in our own image.
Help us as we allow your divine image
　　to define and shape us.
Speak mercy and grace to us,
　　when we deny the path before us,
　　　　and guide us with your shepherding love,
　　　　　　when we are unsure of how to follow.
Strengthen us and give us the courage to say:
　　"Here I am, ready to love and serve."
In your holy name, we pray. Amen.

Words of Assurance (Exod 3, Gen 1)
We are in the presence of the Holy One,
　　whose holiness is in our very being.
Rejoice and be glad, for in Christ's love
　　we are reminded of this divine truth:
　　We are God's beloved creation,
　　reclaimed for a holy path.

Passing the Peace of Christ (Exod 3, Rom 12)
We are standing on holy ground, in the presence of
God's holy children. In recognition of the holy beauty
all around us, share signs of peace and love with one
another.

Response to the Word (Exod 3, Matt 16)

> Holy God, as we sit in this moment of sacred worship,
>> breathe your Holy Spirit within us.
> Speak to us in the silence.
> *(Pause for a time of silence.)*
> Reveal your presence in the fire of love
>> that burns in our own spirits.
> Show us your holy path,
>> that we may move forward
>>> in confidence and courage.

Thanksgiving and Communion

Invitation to the Offering (Exod 3)

> Offering our gifts to God is a holy act. In this sacred moment, let us offer our gifts and our lives to the holy work of God.

Offering Prayer (Exod 3, Rom 12)

> In gratitude for your amazing works in the world,
>> we offer our gifts to further your work, Holy One.
> Bless us as you blessed Moses before us,
>> that we may be a blessing of your holy work.
> Guide our steps, and bless the offerings we bring,
>> that the world may be touched by your holy love.
> Amen.

Sending Forth

Benediction (Exod 3, Rom 12)

God sends us to serve.
> **Here I am, ready to serve!**

God sends us to love.
> **Here I am, ready to love!**

God sends us to bless the world.
> **Here I am, ready to bless the world!**

September 6, 2020

Fourteenth Sunday after Pentecost, Proper 18
B. J. Beu
Copyright © B. J. Beu

Color

Green

Scripture Readings

Exodus 12:1-14; Psalm 149 (or 148); Romans 8, 13:8-14; Matthew 18:15-20

Theme Ideas

Love and judgment focus today's readings. In Exodus, God's love for the Hebrew people leads to God's judgment against their Egyptian slaveholders—an act commemorated in the institution of the Passover celebration. In Psalm 149, God's love for the weak and the helpless leads to God's judgment against unjust kings and nobles—an act that leads to the psalmist's call to celebrate God's salvation with music. In Romans, Paul speaks about the commandment to love as a fulfillment of the law. In Matthew, Jesus's protocol for dealing with sin in the church ensures that future reconciliation will not be encumbered by gossip from unaffected parties.

Invitation and Gathering

Centering Words (Ps 149)

The love of God brings peace to our lives. The judgment of God brings peace to our world.

Call to Worship (Ps 149)

Praise the Lord!
Sing to the Lord a new song.
Let all God's children rejoice.
Clap your hands and praise God with dancing.
Shout for joy and praise God with music.
For God brings justice to the peoples.
God brings judgment upon the powerful.
Sing to the Lord a new song.
Let all God's children rejoice.

—*Or*—

Call to Worship (Rom 13)

Have you heard the good news?
Christ calls us to be people of light.
Have you felt the good news?
Christ offers us God's love and grace.
Have you lived the good news?
Christ lives in us when we gather in his name.
Come! Let us worship the Lord.

Opening Prayer (Exod 12, Ps 149, Rom 13)

God of love and judgment,
when the Egyptians enslaved your people,
your love set them free;
when rulers oppress the poor and powerless,
your judgment brings peace and justice
to the land.

Reach our minds, O God,
>that we may fulfill your law of love.
Touch our hearts, Holy One,
>that we may love our neighbors
>>as we love ourselves. Amen.

Proclamation and Response

Prayer of Yearning (Gen 29, Rom 8)
Merciful God, help us become the people
>you have created us to be.
We yearn to build communities of love,
>but it is easier to tear down than to build up.
We long for the healing of the nations,
>but it is easier to harm than to heal.
We want to bear our grief with dignity,
>but it is satisfying to parade our wounds
>>for all to see.
Bind up our spirits, Gracious One,
>that we might reconcile with those
>>who have caused us pain.
Help us cast aside the things that chain our spirits,
>that we might be free to care for one another
>>and fulfill your law of love. Amen.

Words of Assurance (Matt 18:20 NRSV, Rom 13)
Hear the words of Jesus:
>"Where two or three are gathered in my name,
I am there among them."
As we gather to fulfill the law of love,
>Christ is here to make us whole.

Passing the Peace of Christ (Rom 13)

The night is long gone. Let us take up our work as children of light by sharing signs of Christ's peace with one another.

Response to the Word (Rom 13)

Morning has dawned.
Christ's light shines upon us.
It's time to wake up to the power of love.
For salvation is nearer to us now
than when we first came to believe.
Lay aside the works of darkness
and put on the armor of light.
It's time to wake up to the glory of God.

Thanksgiving and Communion

Offering Prayer (Rom 8, Matt 13)

In celebration of their deliverance from slavery,
the Hebrew people offered you their worship
and their praise.
May the offering we bring before you this day
be a sign of our celebration of your saving love
and your never-failing grace.
Just as Passover stands as a perpetual observance
of your love and care,
so may our weekly offering
be a perpetual observance
of your love in our lives. Amen.

Sending Forth

Benediction (Ps 149)

God has put a new song in our hearts.

We go to sing a new song to the Lord.

God has put a song of justice and peace in our souls.

We go to bring a new song to the world.

God has put a song of joy in our very being.

We go to live a new song with every step we take.

September 13, 2020

Fifteenth Sunday after Pentecost, Proper 19
B. J. Beu

Color

Green

Scripture Readings

Exodus 14:19-31; 15:1b-11, 20-21; Romans 14:1-12;
Matthew 18:21-35

Theme Ideas

Rescue and rejoicing tie today's Exodus readings together. Forgiveness and refraining from judgment tie today's epistle and Gospel readings together. Redemption and reclamation further unify the Exodus and epistle readings—for both are God's gifts to the Hebrew people, just as they are Christ's gifts to the Christian community. In the Exodus story, God rescues the people from Pharaoh, and Miriam leads the rejoicing of her people. God redeems the Israelites from slavery and claims them as the people of God. Likewise, in the epistle to the Romans, Christ redeems us and claims us as God's own children.

Invitation and Gathering

Centering Words *(Exod 14, 15)*

Sing to our God, who brings us into a future of hope
and life.

Call to Worship *(Exod 14, 15, Rom 14)*

Sing of God's mercy and grace.
   Sing of God's strength and might.
Praise God with laughter and joy.
   Praise God with feasting and dance.
For God protects the lowly
and avenges the misdeeds of the mighty.
   God brings forth justice and righteousness,
   saving the weak from the cruelty of the powerful.
Sing of God's mercy and grace.
   Sing of God's strength and might.

Opening Prayer *(Exod 14, 15, Rom 14)*

Gracious God, renew our minds
   with the power of your Holy Spirit.
Cleanse our spirits
   with the mercy of your grace.
Bring us into fellowship with one another
   and grant us courage to defend the lowly.
Part the waters of our troubled thoughts,
   that we might see others as you see them.
Protect us with your powerful hand,
   that we might sing of your faithfulness
      and dance to your glory. Amen.

Proclamation and Response

Prayer of Confession (Exod 14, 15, Rom 14)
>Merciful God, we are ever in need
>>of your grace and your mercy.
>
>When we have injured your little ones,
>>forgive us.
>
>When we have laughed at others' misfortunes,
>>pardon us.
>
>When we have belittled the weak,
>>humble us.
>
>Help us walk the trials of life
>>with your powerful hope
>>>and your loving grace. Amen.

Words of Assurance (Exod 14, 15)
>If it had not been the Lord who was on our side,
>>the forces of death would have devoured us whole.
>
>If it had not been the Lord who was on our side,
>>we would have fallen to the sword
>>or been drowned by the sea.
>
>Dance and sing to the Lord,
>>who is on the side of all God's children.

Passing the Peace (Exod 14, 15, Rom 14)
>The one who rescues us from perishing calls us into fellowship this day. Let us give thanks for the love of God, as we share signs of Christ's peace with one another.

Response to the Word (Exod 14, 15, Rom 14)
>Guide our steps through the waters of fear, Holy One,
>>and lead us to your promised salvation.
>
>As we rejoice in our deliverance,
>>open our mouths with laughter and song.

But let the destruction of those who would hurt us
  fill our eyes with tears,
  for they too are your children.
As faithful followers of Christ,
  may we live as people of promise—
  people bound together in your peace. Amen.

Thanksgiving and Communion

Invitation to the Offering (Exod 14, 15)
With hearts filled with song, let us bring forth our gifts and offer Christ our very lives, that God might work miracles of hope through our giving and our living.

Offering Prayer (Exod 14, Rom 14)
Merciful God, transform this offering
  into hope and joy for a troubled world.
Receive the blessings we return to you this day,
  and transform our ministries
    into instruments of your grace.
Through our giving,
  may places of sorrow and mourning
    know the sound of love and laughter.
Through our living,
  mold us into your people—
    a people of promise and hope,
    a people who live and die in the Lord.

Sending Forth

Benediction (Exod 14, Rom 14)
As you go forth from this place,
plunge into the waters of life unafraid,
for God goes with us.
Move forward in life with purpose and passion,
for Christ is our guide and guardian.
Live as people of powerful hope,
for the Spirit renews us each and every day.
Go with God's blessings.

September 20, 2020

Sixteenth Sunday after Pentecost, Proper 20
Mary Scifres
Copyright © Mary Scifres

Color

Green

Scripture Readings

Exodus 16:2-15; Psalm 105:1-6, 37-45;
Philippians 1:21-30; Matthew 20:1-16

Theme Ideas

Standing firm in faith is a challenging call that every
follower must answer. Whether wandering hungry in
the desert, working faithfully in God's vineyard, or
striving to live in Christian community, we discover
that standing firm isn't as easy as it sounds. Yet today's
letter to the Philippians calls us to do just that. We are
called to live in a manner worthy of Christ's gospel
and of God's grace. To stand firm, we must stand with
one another and with God. That is a challenge worth
accepting!

Invitation and Gathering

Centering Words (Phil 1)

United in one spirit, we are called to stand strongly. United in one mind, we are called to live faithfully. United in one God, we are called to love abundantly.

Call to Worship (Phil 1)

Stand firm, children of God.
We come to serve the Lord.
Stand firm, children of God.
We come to stand in unity and love.
Stand firm, children of God.
We come to live faithfully and fully in Christ.

Opening Prayer (Phil 1)

Love through us, living God,
in the power of your Holy Spirit.
Love through us, Holy One,
by the grace of your child, Jesus Christ.
Strengthen our faith,
that we may respond with trust and hope.
In your mighty name, we pray. Amen.

Proclamation and Response

Prayer of Confession (Exod 16, Phil 1)

Forgive us, Mighty God,
when we doubt your strength.
Assure us, Faithful God,
when we doubt your constant presence.
Renew us, Loving God,
when we neglect to love others
as you have loved us.

Empower us with your strength,
and encourage us with your steadfast love.
Unite us through the power of your Holy Spirit,
that we might live with a faith that honors you,
and abide with a hope that encourages others
to know your love and grace.

Words of Assurance (Phil 1)
Christ's grace makes us whole,
and the Spirit's presence makes us one.
Thanks be to God for these wonderful gifts!

Passing the Peace of Christ (Phil 1)
United in one mind and spirit, let us share signs of love
and peace with one another.

Introduction to the Word (Ps 105)
Dwell on God's wonderful works.
Seek to hear God's voice.
Listen for stories of God's grace.

Response to the Word (Exod 16, Phil 1)
Trust the promises of God.
We stand firm on the foundation of Christ.
Trust God's constant presence.
We stand firm on the foundation of Christ.
Live to serve God.
We stand firm on the foundation of Christ.
Live to love others.
We stand firm on the foundation of Christ.
Live united as a community of faith.
We stand firm on the foundation of Christ.

Thanksgiving and Communion

Invitation to the Offering (Ps 105, Phil 1)

God has generously blessed us and granted us the privilege of sharing our blessings with others. Thanks be to God for this sacred trust.

Offering Prayer (Exod 16, Ps 105)

As we remember your wonderful works,
>we are grateful for your many blessings,
>>and are honored to return these gifts to you.
As we return these gifts to you,
>bless them and send them forth,
>>that others may be showered
>>>with your love and your grace.
In faithful trust, we pray. Amen.

Invitation to Communion (Exod 16, Ps 105)

As God gave our ancestors manna in the wilderness,
>so now God offers us sustenance in this gift
>of holy communion.
Come to be fed.
Come to be filled.
Come to be satisfied with the grace of Christ's love.

Communion Prayer (Phil 1)

Pour out your Holy Spirit on us,
>and on these gifts of bread and wine.
May they be for us your gracious love
>and your abiding presence,
>>that we may be your presence
>>>and your love in the world.
Through the power of your Holy Spirit,
>unite us in one spirit and mind,

and strengthen us for the journey of faith,
to be one with you,
united in ministry to all your world.
Through your child, Jesus Christ,
with the Holy Spirit in your holy church,
all honor and glory is yours, almighty God,
now and forever. Amen.

Sending Forth

Benediction ✓

Go forth with the strength of the Holy Spirit.
Love with the grace of Jesus Christ.
Rejoice in the steadfast love of God.

September 27, 2020

Seventeenth Sunday after Pentecost, Proper 21
B. J. Beu
Copyright © B. J. Beu

Color

Green ✓

Scripture Readings

Exodus 17:1-7; Psalm 78:1-4, 12-16; Philippians 2:1-13;
Matthew 21:23-32

Theme Ideas

The saying: "You had to be there to believe it" is an apt
caption for today's Hebrew Scripture readings. The
power of God is a fearful thing. Memories of God's
mighty deeds of power are passed down in dark sayings of old, so says the psalmist. How do you convey
the wonder and terror of water gushing from a rock on
the mountain of God, simply because Moses struck the
rock with his staff? How do you convey the terror of
a stiff-necked people who walked between the dangers
of death from hunger and thirst in the wilderness and
death from snake bite at the hand of a God angered
by their contemptuous lack of faith? God's power and

authority are not hidden from those who have eyes to see and ears to hear. Yet we often shut our eyes and close our ears to the truth before us, as the chief priests and elders did in the presence of John the Baptist and Jesus. Philippians explains that Christ's power and authority came from his self-emptying and his willingness to become a servant for all. When we answer the call to serve, we do so by God's authority.

Invitation and Gathering

Centering Words
Listen to parables and dark sayings of old. Ponder the stories of Jesus and God's mighty deeds of power.

Call to Worship (Ps 78)
Give ear to God's teaching.
> **We gather to hear the stories of our ancestors.**

Incline your ears to parables and dark sayings of old.
> **We come seeking stories**
> **of God's wondrous power.**

Tell the coming generations of God's glorious deeds.
> **We will not hide them from our children.**

Come to the fount of living water.
> **We will drink deeply from the waters of life.**
> **Taste the wellspring of our salvation.**
> **We gather to worship as people reborn.**

Opening Prayer (Exod 17, Ps 78)
Holy Mystery, the stories of our ancestors
> touch us as dark sayings of old.

Help us behold truths in their stories,
> we are frightened to see in our own.

Open our eyes to see your presence
    amidst their hopes and fears.
Open our hearts to the courage it takes
    to assume leadership in our communities,
        while remaining your faithful followers.
Open our minds to perceive hope
    in the midst of despair.
We believe, Great Spirit.
    Help our unbelief.

Proclamation and Response

Prayer of Yearning (Exod 17, Ps 78, Phil 2, Matt 21)
    God of second chances, you are always there for us.
    In the midst of our grumbling,
        we yearn to find the strength of our convictions.
    In the course of our struggles,
        we long to soldier humbly on,
            forsaking positions of power and authority.
    We want to work gladly in your vineyard,
        without thought of reward or acknowledgement.
    Renew us in your compassion and grace,
        that our eyes may be opened to your presence
            and our minds may be filled
                with the very mind of Christ. Amen.

Words of Assurance (Ps 78, Matt 21)
    Hear the good news:
        No matter who you are,
        or what you have done,
        Christ welcomes us into God's kingdom
        with open arms.
    When we open our hearts and our lives to Christ,
        God's forgiveness is truly ours.

Passing the Peace of Christ (Phil 2)

Be of the same mind, have the same love, and be in full accord with one another, as you turn to one another and share signs of Christ's unity and peace.

Response to the Word (Exod 17)

Ponder ancient parables and dark sayings of old.
We will meditate on the stories of Jesus
and God's mighty deeds of power.
Consider well the fate of those who doubt our God.
We will heed the word of God
and taste the wellspring of our salvation.

Thanksgiving and Communion

Invitation to the Offering (Phil 2)

It's easy to look to our own interests, but God calls us to look to the interests of others. For in so doing, we share the mind of Christ. Let us dedicate ourselves to lives of generosity and service, as we collect today's offering.

Offering Prayer (Exod 17, Phil 2)

God of overflowing abundance,
when your people suffered from thirst,
you satisfied their need
with water from a rock.
Receive our gifts this day, O God,
and transform our gifts into blessing
that grace the lives of others
like an ever-flowing streams.
Receive our thanks and our praise,
our industry and our love,
that all might share your manifold blessings.
Amen.

Sending Forth

Benediction (Phil 2)

> Go to share encouragement in Christ.
> Go to offer consolation in love.
> Go to spread the gifts of the Spirit.
> Go to make God's joy complete.
> Do these things and you will truly live.

October 4, 2020

Eighteenth Sunday after Pentecost, Proper 22
World Communion Sunday

B. J. Beu

Copyright © B. J. Beu

Color

Green

Scripture Readings

Exodus 20:1-4, 7-9, 12-20; Psalm 19; Philippians 3:4b-14;
Matthew 21:33-46

Theme Ideas

The psalmist reminds us that the heavens proclaim God's
glory. And despite the perfection of God's laws, we live
our lives in ignorance. In Exodus, Moses presents the
Hebrew people with the ten commandments, and they
respond in fear. Even Paul, who walked blamelessly under the law, persecuted the church until he recognized
who he was actually persecuting. In Matthew's Gospel,
Jesus tells a parable about slaves killing the master's
son, as a way of foretelling his own rejection and condemnation by God's people. And yet, the heavens continue to proclaim God's glory, working together in all of
creation's majesty to continually proclaim God's handi-
work. We could learn much by listening to the heavens.

Invitation and Gathering

Centering Words (Ps 19)

The heavens declare the glory of God, and the seas roar
the wonder of the Lord.

Call to Worship (Ps 19)

The heavens are telling the glory of God.
The skies proclaim the work of God's hands.
Day and night return endlessly,
showing God's steadfast love.
The sun shines upon the earth,
reflecting God's light.
The law of God is perfect, reviving the soul.
The decrees of God bring wisdom,
making wise the pure of heart.
The heavens are telling the glory of God.
The skies proclaim the work of God's hands.
Come! Let us worship the living God.

Opening Prayer (Exod 20)

God of majesty and mystery,
we stand huddled at the base of the mountain,
as you pour forth your power
and your splendor.
Though we seek your guidance,
we shake with fear
when you meet us face to face.
Bless us with your commandments,
and teach us the ways of life and death,
that we may be a people
worthy of your loving care. Amen.

Opening Prayer (Matt 21)

> Cornerstone of our faith, do not abandon us
> > when we fall away from you.
> You are the true master of the vineyard;
> > we are here to work in your fields
> > > and make disciples throughout the world.
> Bring us into your kingdom,
> > that we might taste the sweetness of your mercy
> > > and share the joy of your grace. Amen.

Proclamation and Response

Prayer of Confession (Phil 3)

> Holy God, like Paul before us,
> > we have ignored Wisdom's cries.
> We have blinded ourselves to your truth
> > and trusted our blurred vision.
> We have put our faith in our own righteousness,
> > rather than in the righteousness of your Son.
> We have persecuted others out of ignorance
> > and willful misunderstanding.
> Help us forsake our pride,
> > that we might have life,
> > > and have it abundantly. Amen.

Assurance of Pardon (Phil 3)

> The one who created us, seeks us still,
> > beckoning us into union with Christ.
> Seek God and receive acceptance in Christ's name.

Passing the Peace of Christ (Ps 19)

> The heavens are telling the glory of God. Let us share in
> the joy of their heavenly song, as we exchange signs of
> Christ's peace with one another.

Introduction to the Word (Exod 20)

God is calling from the mountain top.
We wait for God's saving word.
God brings us commandments to live by,
that we may be a godly people.
We wait to be transformed by God's word.
Worship God alone. Make no graven idols.
Do not take the Lord's name in vain.
Keep the Sabbath holy. Honor your father and mother.
We will keep God's holy commandments.
Do not murder. Be faithful to your loved ones.
Do not steal or bear false witness against another.
And do not covet the things you do not have.
We will hear the lessons that God teaches.

Response to the Word (Matt 21)

The cornerstone that the builders rejected
is our foundation and our strength.
Christ, we build our lives on you.
Those who turn from God and forsake God's ways
labor in vain.
Christ, we set our hearts on you.
The ways of life are hidden from the unrighteous.
Christ, we place our hopes on you.

Thanksgiving and Communion

Offering Prayer (Exod 20)

God of never-failing love,
you call us from the clouds of your glory
to teach us the ways of life and death.
When your people suffered from thirst,
you satisfied their need with water from a rock.

Receive our gifts this day, O God,
>that they may satisfy the needs of your people today
>>like water from an ever-flowing stream.
Receive our thanks and our praise,
>our industry and our love,
>>that all might know your manifold blessings.
Amen.

Invitation to Communion

This is the feast of God's goodness.
>**Let us break bread together.**
This is the Sabbath of our souls.
>**Let us break bread together.**
This is the promise of resurrection and life.
>**Let us break bread together.**
This is the gift of Christ's love for us.
>**Let us break bread together.**

Prayer of Thanksgiving

Promise of salvation,
>thank you for this gift of grace.
As we gather at your table and eat of this bread,
>nourish us with the truth of your word
>>and the blessing of your covenant.
As we drink of this cup and share table together,
>fill us with the hope of your salvation.
Remind us that we are one body in your name
>with your disciples throughout time and history.
May our lives proclaim the mystery and majesty
>of your saving grace. Amen.

Sending Forth

Benediction (Exod 20, Ps 19)

Listen, the mountain of God thunders.
>   **We will live in God's ways**
>   **and share God's teachings with the world.**

Listen, the heavens proclaim God's glory.
>   **God has blessed us with the path of holy love.**

Go with God.

—Or—

Benediction (Matt 21)

Go with the blessings of the one who understands
>   our trials and tribulations.

Go with the blessings of the cornerstone of our faith.

October 11, 2020

Nineteenth Sunday after Pentecost, Proper 23
Mary Scifres
Copyright © Mary Scifres

Color

Green ✓

Scripture Readings

Exodus 32:1-14; Psalm 106:1-6, 19-23; Philippians 4:1-9;
Matthew 22:1-14

Theme Ideas

because Here is.

We are partners in ministry and creation with God.
Whether Moses is pleading for the lives of the Hebrew
people, or Paul is pleading with the Philippians to turn to
God and to one another for fullness of ministry and joy,
today's scriptures illustrate the power of partnering with
God. Jesus presents an image of a wedding banquet that
can be truly joy-filled only when everyone participates,
from the greatest to the least, in full partnership with
God. Moses reminds God of the divine partnership with
the Hebrew people and convinces God not to destroy
them when they fall short of God's expectation. We too
are given chances to change God's mind. Even if we're

not Moses, we are all in a partnership with God. Being created in God's divine image gives us a unique role and a powerful call to participate fully with the Holy One.

Invitation and Gathering

Centering Words (Phil 4, James 4:8)
    Draw near to God, and God will draw near to us, as we
    serve and minister together.

Call to Worship (Exod 32, Phil 4, Matt 22)
    Invited by God,
      we gather to worship.
    Partnering with God,
      we gather to grow in faith
      and to change the world.

Opening Prayer (Phil 4, Matt 22)
    Beloved God, we gather in the shelter of your love,
      grateful for the banquet of worship
        you have prepared for us.
    Focus our hearts and our minds
      on the beauty of this time,
        the blessings of our lives,
          and the fullness of your message.
    Strengthen our call to fulfill our role
      as your partners in ministry to the world. Amen.

Proclamation and Response

Prayer of Confession (Matt 22)
    Gracious God, you know how we confuse our roles,
      miss your invitation,

and ignore your banquet of grace
and abundant love.
Clear the clouds from our eyes,
that we may clearly see clearly
your call to partner and serve with you.
Clear our calendars,
that we don't miss your invitation
to love and serve the world.
Clear our minds and soothe our troubled souls,
that we may remember and treasure
the opportunity to receive your abundant
grace and your loving nourishment.
Nourish us with your forgiveness and your mercy,
that we may rejoice fully in this time of worship.
In your love and grace, we pray. Amen.

Words of Assurance (Phil 4)

Rejoice in God, whose grace is ours.
Rejoice in the power of love!

Passing the Peace

We are blessed by a peace that passes all understanding,
a grace that transcends all logic, and a love that breaks
all bounds. With joy, let us share these amazing gifts, as
we greet one another this day.

Response to the Word (Exod 32, Phil 4)

Called apart to serve God alone,
we are ready to focus on what is good and true.
Called to be partners with God,
we are ready to serve God and God's world.
Called as beloved children of the Most High,
we are ready to love, as we have been loved.
Called by God,
we are blessed indeed.

Thanksgiving and Communion

Invitation to the Offering (Phil 4)
> Come with thanksgiving, to offer your gifts and honor
> to God.

Offering Prayer (Phil 4, Matt 22)
> Gracious God, thank you for your abundant love
>> and your nourishing grace.
> Thank you for the gifts we return to you now.
> Bless these gifts,
>> that they may become for others
>>> signs of your abundant love
>>>> and vessels of your nourishing grace.
> Amen.

Sending Forth

Benediction (Phil 4)
> As partners with God,
> go to serve God's world.
> As friends of Christ,
> go to share Christ's love.
>> **We go with the blessing of God,**
>> **the strength of Jesus Christ,**
>> **and the guidance of the Holy Spirit.**

October 18, 2020

Twentieth Sunday after Pentecost, Proper 24
Mary Sue Brookshire

Color

Green

Scripture Readings

Exodus 33:12-23; Psalm 99; 1 Thessalonians 1:1-10; Matthew 22:15-22

Theme Ideas

God is holy, set apart, and beyond our comprehension. And yet, God is as close as our next breath, intimately connected with us and knowable to us. As people of faith, we sometimes have trouble holding these two truths in tension with each other. The texts for today speak both of God's glory and majesty as well as God's deep love and concern for us. Created by God, we bear God's image. Through the power of the Holy Spirit, we become imitators of God—visible signs of God's presence with us.

Invitation and Gathering

Centering Words (Exod 33, Ps 99, 1 Thess 1)
As we gather today, God is with us. The Holy One knows us. The Living God shines through us.

Call to Worship (Exod 33, Ps 99, 1 Thess 1, Matt 22)
Brothers and sisters, we are loved by God.
The ruler of heaven and earth knows us by name.
God hears and answers our cries for help.
God shows compassion and kindness to us.
May our lives praise and magnify
our great and awesome God.
**We have come to worship the one whose image
is imprinted within us.**

Opening Prayer (Exod 33, Ps 99, 1 Thess 1)
Magnificent and Holy One, we long to know you better.
As we make our way in this world,
we search for signs that you are with us.
Give us a glimpse of your glorious presence,
and show us your ways.
May our lives ring out the marvelous message
of your goodness, your mercy, and your love. Amen.

Proclamation and Response

Prayer of Confession (Exod 33, Ps 99, 1 Thess 1, Matt 22)
O God, our God, you have shown us your ways
and promised to walk with us.
Through your Son, Jesus,
you have given us an example to follow,
that we might be imitators of your divine love.

But we have not kept the laws and rules
    you have given us.
Lover of justice,
    forgive us when we forget whose image we bear.
May the deep convictions of our faith
    be displayed through acts of kindness,
        compassion and mercy,
            in your holy name we pray. Amen.

Words of Assurance (Exod 33, Ps 99)

Our God is a God who forgives,
    showing kindness and compassion to all.
When we call on God, God hears and answers us.
Through Jesus Christ, we are forgiven.

Passing the Peace of Christ (1 Thess 1:4)

"Brothers and sisters, you are loved by God!" In this hope and promise, exchange signs of peace, and greet one another with this good news.

Response to the Word (Exod 33, Ps 99, 1 Thess 1, Matt 22)

As ones who bear God's image,
    we are called to be imitators
    of the one who loves justice.
Through Jesus Christ, God has shown us God's ways.
When we follow him with faithfulness,
    the good news of God's love rings out from us!

Thanksgiving and Communion

Invitation to the Offering (Matt 22)

"Give to Caesar what belongs to Caesar and to God what belongs to God." With gratitude for all we have received, we offer our gifts to God.

Offering Prayer (Matt 22)
These offerings represent only a part
of what we owe you.
Our currency bears the imprint of worldly powers,
but we bear the holy image
you inscribe on our hearts.
All that we have and all that we are
belong to you, O God.
As we give these gifts and ourselves freely to you,
may others know your goodness and your love,
through our offerings. Amen.

Sending Forth

Benediction (Exod 33, 1 Thess 1, Matt 22)
Go now to serve the living God,
whose image we bear.
We go, knowing that God goes with us.
May all our work be done with faith.
May all our efforts be filled with love.
Go and persevere with the hope
that comes through Jesus Christ.

October 25, 2020

Twenty-First Sunday after Pentecost, Proper 25
Reformation Sunday

B. J. Beu

Color

Green

Scripture Readings

Deuteronomy 34:1-12; Psalm 90:1-6, 13-17;
1 Thessalonians 2:1-8; Matthew 22:34-46

Theme Ideas

Good works are no guarantee of good fortune. God takes Moses up a mountain to see the promised land—a land Moses will never reach. The psalmist pleads with God to grant the people a year of blessing and peace for every year they have suffered evil. Paul brings the gospel to the Thessalonians despite his terrible treatment at Philippi. Despite seeking to teach us the ways of life, Jesus suffers question and scorn from those who seek to discredit him. And still, we are called to remain faithful, to love God and our neighbors as ourselves.

Invitation and Gathering

Centering Words (Matt 22)

When we love God and our neighbors, everything changes.

Call to Worship (Ps 90)

With hearts ready to serve,
> **God turns our mourning into singing**
> **and our sorrows into laughter.**

With hope and expectation,
> **God turns our weeping into celebration**
> **and our grief into shouts of joy .**

Come before the Lord with yearning,
with hearts ready to serve.

Opening Prayer (Ps 90)

Eternal Mystery,
> before the mountains were brought forth,
>> and the seas began to roar,
>>> you are God.

You make us like grass,
> which flourishes in the morning
>> and fades in the evening.

In the blink of an eye,
> we turn back to dust,
>> for a thousand years in your sight
>> are like a watch in the night.

Restore us, O Lord,
> and heal us with your saving love,
>> for we are your people,
>>> and you are our God. Amen.

—Or—

Opening Prayer (Ps 90)

> Bless your servants, O God,
> > and favor us with your steadfast love.
> May your love flow through us
> > like springs of living water,
> > > that we may rejoice and be glad
> > > > all our days of our lives. Amen.

Proclamation and Response

Prayer of Yearning (Matt 22)

> May your love, Eternal God,
> > move all that stands before it.
> We yearn to love our neighbors
> > as we love ourselves,
> > > but often find such love beyond us.
> Nurture us in your healing love,
> > that fear may hold no sway over us.
> Amen.

Words of Assurance (1 Thess 2)

> God commands us to fulfill the law of love
> > by loving we have been loved.
> In fulfilling the law of love,
> > we fulfill the law and the prophets.
> In fulfilling the law of love,
> > we find forgiveness and peace.

Passing the Peace of Christ (1 Thess 2, Matt 22)

> By fulfilling the law of love, we are brought into unity
> with Christ and with one another. Let us celebrate this
> unity by sharing signs of Christ's peace with one another.

Response to the Word (1 Thess 2)
> If God's word is not to be heard in vain,
>> let us declare the gospel
>>> to a world in need of good news.
> Even when faced with opposition and derision,
>> let us be as gentle in our instruction,
>>> as a mother who cares for her children.
> Help us share the good news we have heard this day,
>> with a world in need of your love.

Thanksgiving and Communion

Offering Prayer (Matt 22:37-39 NRSV)
> We have heard what we must do:
>> "You shall love the Lord your God
>>> with all your heart, and with all your soul,
>>> and with all your mind.
>> And ... you shall love your neighbor as yourself."
> May the offerings we bring this day
>> be a sign of our commitment
>>> to be known by our love.
> Bless these offerings and our loving
>> in your holy name, we pray. Amen.

Sending Forth

Benediction (Matt 22)
> God's love sends us forth.
> **God's love sets us free.**
> God's love makes us whole.
> **God's love brings us hope.**
> God's love blesses our lives.
> **God's love brings healing to our world.**

November 1, 2020

All Saints' Day
Beryl A. Ingram

Color

White

Scripture Readings

Revelation 7:9-17; 1 John 3:1-3; Psalm 34:1-10, 22;
Matthew 5:1-12

Theme Ideas

All Saints Day conjures images of that great cloud of
witnesses gathered so near to us that it creates palpable
energy. Revelation pictures saints from every place and
time—everyone is there—singing in the presence of God.
First John gives us a glimpse of what is in store for us
as we go on to perfection, filled increasingly with God.
Psalm 34 invites us to praise God, whose goodness is
beyond our comprehension. The Beatitudes (or BE-Atti-
tudes) in Matthew affirm those who are marginalized by
humility, sorrow, care-giving, longing for right relationships with God and neighbor, and even living the gospel
of Jesus Christ. For what appears weak or impoverished
to the world actually touches the heart of God. As we allow God to direct more and more of our life-choices, we
grow in holiness as we are filled with love.

Invitation and Gathering

Centering Words

Let the saints sing for joy. We are children of the living God. We will see God face to face.

Call to Worship (Rev 7)

As we gather, we remember that we are not alone!
We gather with the saints,
who live in the presence of God,
singing praises to the God of our salvation.
From every nation, race, clan and culture,
God's people gather to worship
the One-Who-Is-Without-Peer!
To God and to the Lamb, all honor, glory,
wisdom, thanksgiving, strength and power.
Blessed be God, now and forever! Amen!
Amen!

—Or—

Call to Worship (Ps 34)

Let us bless God every chance we get.
We bless the God of our salvation.
Magnify the Lord.
We lift up God's name in praise.
O taste and see that God is good.
Those who make their home in God
are filled with joy.
Magnify the Lord.
Lift God's name in praise.

Opening Prayer (Ps 34, Matt 5)

Blessed are you, God of our salvation.
As we turn to you in prayer,
be with us and reveal to us your ways

From your self-revelation in Jesus
> teach us how to live in ways that honor you:
>> by humbling ourselves;
>> by being content with what we have
>>> rather than striving for more;
>> by caring, and cooperating,
>>> rather than competing in unhealthy ways.

Teach us, giver of all goodness,
> to be strong in your strength
>> for the sake of the gospel.

Help us honor your prodigal grace,
> by living as doers of peace
>> in this world you love. Amen

Proclamation and Response

Prayer of Confession

Holy God, we so often fail to remember
how profoundly you love us.
> **You bless us even when we are at our wit's end.**

You created us, and you love us as we are,
even as you inspire our desire to be better
through your Holy Spirit.
> **Forgive us when we fail to remember**
> **that we are the body of Christ,**
> **saints-in-process.**

Empower us to begin anew,
encouraged by the stories of those
who live in your eternal presence.
> **In the name of Jesus,**
> **and for the sake of the gospel,**
> **we pray. Amen**

Words of Assurance

Beloved, we are the children of God.
Don't fear failure.
It is endemic to our human nature.
Learn from your mistakes,
    and cherish the forgiving grace of God.
Give thanks for all you are, and go forward in faith,
    knowing that God is faithful.

Response to the Word (Matt 5)

You are blessed when your last option fails.
    For without the gift of failure,
    our vision will not clear to see new possibilities;
    our eyes will not be able to see the God
    who is there for us in new, life-giving ways.
You are blessed when you care for others
and when you are kind and compassionate.
    As we are to others, God will be to us.
You are blessed when your heart is filled with God.
    As others see God in us,
    we will see God everywhere.
You are blessed when you choose non-violence
as your response of choice.
    As we seek good for others,
    rather than harm for them,
    others will recognize the God-within-us.
You are blessed when you live for God
and people despise you and turn on you
for your kingdom choices.
    When we live for God,
    despite the persecution it brings,
    we find ourselves in holy company—
    saints and prophets and all who love God.

**We find ourselves with Jesus
standing next to us, smiling.**

Thanksgiving and Communion

Offering Prayer (Rev 7)

Holy God, thank you for the great cloud of witnesses
that surrounds us as we worship.
Their diversity reminds us of your infinite grace
to all your creatures.
Thank you for the vision of a world at peace:
paradise restored, where no one hungers,
no one thirsts, and no one is wanting.
You guide us to the source of living water
and invite us to drink deeply of your love.
Your magnificent generosity
evokes our deepest thanks.
And so receive these offerings,
that we may join that great cloud of witnesses
as we share our gifts with others. Amen.

Sending Forth

Benediction (Ps 34)

We are renewed and filled with the sweetness of God.
Go forth to bless the world with joy
in the Spirit of God's redemptive love
and sustaining peace. Amen.

November 1, 2020

Twenty-Second Sunday after Pentecost, Proper 26
Bryan Schneider-Thomas

Color

Green

Scripture Readings

Joshua 3:7-17; Psalm 107:1-7, 33-37;
1 Thessalonians 2:9-13; Matthew 23:1-12

Theme Ideas

The Gospel lesson is an opportunity to reflect on the broad nature of the Church and the community of God. Within this context, the other scriptures offer insight and commentary. Joshua and Psalm 107 speak of God's abiding presence—a presence that guides this community. First Thessalonians offers a glimpse at the nature of the community founded on God's word. Matthew's Gospel speaks of how we are to act and view ourselves.

Invitation and Gathering

Centering Words (Matt 23:12 NRSV)
God's word calls to us: "All who humble themselves will be exalted."

Call to Worship (Ps 107)

Give thanks to God.

God's steadfast love endures forever.

With holy hands we are protected.

God turns desert wastes into beautiful gardens.

Give thanks to God.

God's steadfast love endures forever.

—Or—

Call to Worship

Through stories of faith and acts of grace,

we are reminded that God is always here.

By God's presence, we are guided.

Through God's word, we are instructed.

With God's Spirit, we are formed.

Come, let us lift our voices in praise,

and offer our lives in service to God.

Opening Prayer (Josh 3)

Almighty God, your abiding presence

guides your people through the wilderness

into the promised land.

Your steadfast love continues to abide with us today,

as we walk as your children,

and as we serve others with Christ's love. Amen.

Proclamation and Response

Responsive Prayer (1 Thess 2)

Holy God, you care for us as a loving parent,

that we might do the same for others.

Help us proclaim and bear witness to the gospel,

that all might recognize your word.

Strengthen us with your grace,
that we might be pure, upright
and blameless before others.
>   **In our churches,**
>   **may your word be taught.**
In our lives,
may your word be seen.
>   **In our world,**
>   **may your word dwell forever. Amen.**

Invitation to the Word
(The following lines may be read before each individual scripture reading or before them collectively.)
Hear the word of God,
>   that you might walk in holiness all your days.
Receive the word of God,
>   that it might be at work within you.
Heed the word of God,
>   that you may become its servant.

Response to the Word (1 Thess 2)
By the word, God calls us into covenant.
>   **May the divine word work within us.**
May we be receptive students of it.
>   **May it show us the call of service**
>   **in Christ's holy Church.**

Thanksgiving and Communion

Invitation to the Offering
As the Church, we are called to serve. Our service begins by offering our lives to Christ, and continues through the gifts we give, that the Church may continue to witness to the word of God.

Offering Prayer

To you, O God, we offer our praise.

For you, we offer our gifts.

With you, we offer our lives in service to the world.

Teach us to embody your word

in action and service,

that we may present ourselves

as living sacrifice to you

and your holy word.

Sending Forth

Benediction

May God's steadfast love keep you from harm

and lead you into Christ's service this week.

November 8, 2020

Twenty-Third Sunday after Pentecost, Proper 27
B. J. Beu

Color

Green

Scripture Readings

Joshua 24:1-3a, 14-25; Psalm 78:1-7;
1 Thessalonians 4:13-18; Matthew 25:1-13

Theme Ideas

Choices have consequences. Choosing to follow God
changes everything. Choosing to share the wisdom of
God's holy mystery with the next generation provides
our children a chance at a real future. Choosing to
remain vigilant keeps us ready when the bridegroom
appears. Today's scriptures remind us that we need per-
sistence, patience, and faithfulness for the long haul. But
first and foremost, they remind us that it all begins with
a choice: Whom will we serve?

Invitation and Gathering

Centering Words (Josh 24, Ps 78)
> What decision would change your life forever? Choosing this day to follow God is that decision. What is stopping you?

Call to Worship (Josh 24, Ps 78, 1 Thess 4)
> Our ancestors have led us here.
>> **We are witnesses of their faith.**
> The wisdom of the ages has called us here.
>> **We are children of its call.**
> The choice to follow God lies before us.
>> **We are heirs of its promise.**
> The Lord of life has called us here.
>> **We are here to worship the Lord.**

Opening Prayer (Josh 24, Ps 78, Matt 25)
> Lord of Life, we come his day
>> to follow the ways you set before us.
> Show us the signs of your coming kingdom,
>> that we may be worthy of our invitation.
> May we have the wisdom
>> to teach our children your ways
>>> and pass on a better world
>>>> to the generations to come. Amen.

Proclamation and Response

Prayer of Yearning (Josh 24, Matt 25)
> We long to have the courage to choose you, O God,
>> each and every day.
> We yearn for the forbearance to wait patiently,

through the long watches of the night—
for we long to be found ready,
when you appear in your glory.
Fill our lamps with your grace,
that we might share your light with our children
and with the generations to come. Amen.

Words of Assurance (1 Thess 4:17 NRSV)

Hold onto these words of hope:
"We will be with the Lord forever."
Love the Lord of life and live.

Passing the Peace of Christ (Josh 24, Matt 25)

Christ offers us peace when we choose life and follow God. Let us celebrate this peace as we share signs
of God's blessings and healing wisdom, each and
every day.

Introduction to the Word (Josh 24, Matt 25)

Listen for the word of God and keep your lamps lit. Listen…hear…receive…choose to let God in.

Response to the Word (Josh 24, Ps 78, 1 Thess 4, Matt 25)

Have you made your choice?
Are you prepared for the journey?
We will walk with God.
We will choose hope over despair.
Have you embraced your choice?
Are you ready to share the lessons you have learned?
We will live our choice.
We will teach our children
the wisdom handed down to us of old.

Thanksgiving and Communion

Invitation to the Offering (Matt 25)

We need oil for our lamps, food for our tables, and love for our lives. Let us share the bounty we have received, that no one may be left out alone in the dark.

Offering Prayer (Josh 24)

We come before you, O God,
    with gifts in your name
        in service of the world.
We bring you this offering,
    as a symbol of our choice to follow you.
Receive these gifts of love,
    that they may go forth as your blessing
        and wisdom for the world. Amen.

Sending Forth

Benediction (Josh 24, Matt 25)

Go forth this day and keep your lamps lit.
We go with hearts ablaze with God's love.
Go forth this day and shine with God's light.
We go with lives kindled with the call to serve.
Go forth this day and enter into fullness of life.
We go to embrace the life we have received.

November 15, 2020

Twenty-Fourth Sunday after Pentecost, Proper 28

B. J. Beu
Copyright © B. J. Beu

Color

Green

Scripture Readings

Judges 4:1-7; Psalm 123; 1 Thessalonians 5:1-11;
Matthew 25:14-30

Theme Ideas

Themes of judgment and redemption unify today's
readings. Judges recounts a familiar pattern: Israel sins,
Israel is delivered by God into the hand of its neighbors
as punishment, Israel repents and returns to God's precepts, then God raises up a judge to rescue Israel. The
psalmist cries out for mercy to a God who hears our
pleas. The epistle warns that the day of the Lord is coming like a thief in the night, but that the righteous have
nothing to fear if they remain vigilant and faithful to
God. Finally, the Gospel recounts Jesus's parable of the
talents and the judgment God metes out based on how
we use our gifts. Here, redemption is tied to steward-
ship—it comes to those who make the most of God's
gifts, those who work for the kingdom.

Invitation and Gathering

Centering Words (Matt 25)

Use the talents you possess, for silent would the forest
be, if the only birds that sang were those who sang the
best.
(paraphrase of quotation attributed to Henry Van Dyke)

Call to Worship (1 Thess 5)

The day of the Lord comes
like a thief in the night.
We will not be caught unaware.
Forsake the ways of darkness.
We will live as children of light.
Put on the breastplate of faith,
and the helmet of salvation.
We will prepare ourselves
for the struggles that lie ahead.
Encourage one another
and build each other up.
We will work for the kingdom
and live as children of light.
Come, let us worship the source of love and light.

—*Or*—

Call to Worship (Matt 25)

God calls us to use our gifts
for the building of God's kingdom.
But we're afraid.
Christ urges us to find our courage
and not look back.
But our gifts seem so small.

The Spirit offers us everything we need.
But what if we fail?
Trust the gifts you have been given.
We will celebrate our gifts
as we worship God this day.

Opening Prayer (1 Thess 5)
God of fall and winter, God of spring and summer,
    you know the seasons of our lives.
Let the season of darkness and doubt pass away,
    that we may be reborn in your light.
Lead us into a season of light and warmth:
    a season of joy;
    a season of sober judgment;
    a season where your children clothe themselves
        in the breastplate of faith and hope,
            and the helmet of hope and salvation.
Help us put aside the ways of darkness
    and live as children of light. Amen.

Proclamation and Response

Prayer of Yearning (Matt 25)
Faithful Steward, you bless us with gifts
    that are uniquely our own.
We long to use the talents you bestow upon us
    to build your kingdom.
We yearn to live with gratitude
    for all that you have done for us
        and the opportunities you place before us.
Clear our vision, Holy One,
    and help us see the good we can do
        with the gifts and talents we have received.
Amen.

Words of Assurance (Matt 25:23 NRSV)
Rejoice, sisters and brothers,
>for our gifts and talents.

Hear these words of assurance:
>"Well done, good and trustworthy [servant];
>>you have been trustworthy in a few things,
>>I will put you in charge of many things;
>>enter into the joy of your master."

Passing the Peace of Christ (1 Thess 5)
Called to live as children of light, let us build one another up as we share signs of peace, and words of love.

Introduction to the Word (Ps 123, 1 Thess 5)
Enthroned in the heavens,
>**God speaks to us on high.**

Hear words of promise and warning
in the bitter watches of the night.
>**We will listen for the word of God,**
>**and live as children of light.**

Response to the Word (1 Thess 5, Matt 25)
What time it is?
>**It's time to wake up.**

What time it is?
>**It's time to get going.**

What time it is?
>**It's time to live as children of light.**

What time it is?
>**It's time to trust God's love**
>**and answer Christ's call!**

Thanksgiving and Communion

Offering Prayer (1 Thess 5, Matt 25)
> Giver of gifts, you bestow us with talents
> > that are far more precious than jewels.
> Open our eyes to the possibilities
> > you hold for our world.
> Transform the gifts we offer this day
> > into light and love for the world.
> Transform our talents into blessings
> > for a world in need. Amen.

Sending Forth

Benediction (1 Thess 5)
> Clothed in faith and showered in love,
> > **we go forth, shining with God's light.**
> Washed in joy and bathed in hope,
> > **we go forth, radiant with Christ's love.**
> Blessed with gifts far more precious than jewels,
> > **we go forth, blazing with the fire of God's Spirit.**

November 22, 2020

Reign of Christ/Christ the King, Proper 29
Mary Scifres
Copyright © Mary Scifres

Color

White

Scripture Readings

Ezekiel 34:11-16, 20-24; Psalm 100; Ephesians 1:15-23; Matthew 25:31-46

Theme Ideas

Being a ruler of sheep is probably not all that kingly a duty, and yet it is the servant-call that Christ has accepted in our lives and in our world. Today's scriptures remind us that caring selflessly is the work of Christ our King, and also the work to which we are called. Power and dominion are not gilded with jewels and palaces. Rather, power and dominion carry great responsibility. To be the name above all names is to be the servant of all humanity. To be those who claim the name "Christian" is to follow our servant-master and become servants to all in need. To see and respond to those needs are the marks of a Christian follower. To care for others, we must open our eyes and see the needs that surround us each and every day.

Invitation and Gathering

Centering Words (Matt 25)

When we care for the poor, clothe the naked, and visit
the sick and imprisoned, we are caring for Christ. When
we love our neighbor, we are really loving God.

Call to Worship (Ps 100, Matt 25)

Make a joyful noise, a noise of love and care!
Praise God with generosity and compassion!
Sing to the Lord with acts of kindness!
Give God glory with missions of mercy!
Make a joyful noise, a noise of love and care!
Praise God with justice and righteousness!

—Or—

Call to Worship (Matt 25)

Sheep and goats are welcome here.
Saints and sinners are part of God's world.
Come; rejoice in Christ Jesus, who welcomes us all.
Come; share in his grace,
that we all might become sheep—
who feed one another,
who show compassion and love,
who offer comfort and mercy,
who give as we have received.
Come; rejoice in Christ Jesus,
who welcomes us all!

Opening Prayer (Eph 1, Matt 25)

Glorious God, shine upon us
with your Spirit of wisdom and truth.
Enlighten our hearts.

Help us to know the hope
>to which we are called.

Reveal your ways,
>that we might share hope and joy
>>in all that we do, and all that we say.

In the light of Christ's love, we pray. Amen.

Proclamation and Response

Prayer of Confession (Matt 25)

God of glory, we do not always see your glory
>in the world around us.

When we see a person in need,
>it is not easy to look him in the eye.

When we hear a cry for help,
>it is not easy to offer her quick assurance.

When we know of a lonely prisoner,
>it is not easy to make that unannounced visit.

Forgive us when we fail to see you
>in our everyday lives.

Forgive us when we are afraid to act,
>afraid to care.

Encourage us, God of glory.

Help us to see others with the eyes of compassion,
>that we might be your loving presence
>>in the world. Amen.

Words of Assurance (Eph 1)

There is immeasurable greatness in the power of God
>for those who believe.

Trust in the Lord,
>for God's grace is real.

In the name of Jesus Christ,
    who is above all and in all,
    you are forgiven!

Response to the Word (Matt 25)
    Compassionate God, help us show compassion
        to everyone we meet.
    Help us see your face:
        in every hungry child,
        in every tired woman,
        in every disappointed man.
    Help us hear your cry:
        in every person who mourns,
        every person who is lonely,
        every person who is in agony.
    Help us feel your presence,
        that we might have the courage and confidence
        to act with compassion and love everywhere we go,
        and with everyone we meet. Amen.

Thanksgiving and Communion

Invitation to the Offering (Ps 100, Matt 25)
    Enter God's gates with thanksgiving and praise.
    Come to the Lord, who is good.
    Let us continue God's faithfulness
        in our acts of giving and works of charity.

Offering Prayer (Matt 25)
    We offer these gifts to you:
        as food and drink for a hungry world;
        as clothing and shelter
            for those who are naked and homeless;
        as kindness and compassion
            for those who are most in need of mercy.

Transform these gifts,
that they might be your hands and feet
in the world.
Send us forth as your people,
that all that we do, and all that we say,
may be a glorious representation
of your presence in the world.
With gratitude, we pray. Amen.

Sending Forth

Benediction (Ezek 34, Matt 25)

Go to seek the lost and bind up the injured.
We will strengthen the weak,
and encourage the fainthearted.
Go to seek justice and love mercy.
We will help the world know the feast
of God's justice and the grace of God's mercy.

November 26, 2020

Thanksgiving Day
Beverly Boke

Color

White

Scripture Readings

Deuteronomy 8:7-18; Psalm 65; 2 Corinthians 9:6-15; Luke 17:11-19

Theme Ideas

The Earth is a gift, an unearned treasure. Our task is to find harmony in our relationship to this good gift. Our actions as individuals and as communities can honor or desecrate the gift. When we forget the blessedness of this creation, we stray from what is good.

Invitation and Gathering

Centering Words
The Earth is a gift, an unearned treasure.

Call to Worship
From Mother Earth, we were formed.
From Mother Earth, we are fed.

From lives of bounty, we are blessed.
 From homes and work, we have gathered here.
Come, eat your fill and bless our God.
 Earth's bounties are given for our nourishment!
Share these gifts and bless our world.
 Earth's bounties are given for all.
(*Mary Scifres*)

Lighting the Candles / Flaming Chalice
 We welcome all who come to give thanks this day;
  all who join with neighbors in glad thanksgiving,
  acknowledging together the bounty of our lives.
 Let this flame rise, signifying our impulse
 toward the Divine.
  Let us rejoice together on this day
  of giving thanks!

Opening Prayer (Deut 8)
 Extravagant, generous giver of all good things,
  just as you brought the Israelites
   into a land flowing with milk and honey—
    a land where they could be free
     from bondage and oppression,
  you have brought us into this good land—
   a land with flowing streams,
    with springs and underground waters
     welling up in valleys and hills,
   a land of wheat and corn, of fertile plains,
   and majestic mountains.
 We give you thanks:
  for the bounty that fills our tables,
  for the water that satisfies our thirst,
  for the beauty of this land

where we are free to worship you
in the name of Jesus, who is the Christ.
Amen.
(Deborah Sokolove)

Proclamation and Response

*Meditation / **Words of Preparation***
Let us always be mindful
that the place where we stand is holy.
This planet is our home, our life, our hope.
Every breath we take receives the whole world.
Every step we take moves us through generations of life.
Matter is neither created nor destroyed;
it is changed endlessly,
and we who affect changes
are bound by our faith to consider
our potential for good and for harm.
Let us be mindful, then, of this great gift—
which we neither made nor earned,
conceived nor understand.
And let us walk in gentleness
upon the great Mother Earth.

Thanksgiving and Communion

Communion Litany
How rich the beauty of the earth!
What wondrous things God has done.
We thank thee, now, O God,
with hearts and hands and voices.

From our mothers' arms, God has blessed us.
From Mother Earth, we are fed and nourished.
> **We thank thee, now, O God,**
> **with hearts and hands and voices.**

Along the way, God is with us,
offering countless gifts of love through the ages.
> **We thank thee, now, O God,**
> **with hearts and hands and voices.**

May God grant grace for our troubled days;
and guidance on the journey of life.
> **We thank thee, now, O God,**
> **with hearts and hands and voices.**

May our abundant God be ever near;
may our hearts be always grateful.
> **We thank thee, now, O God,**
> **with hearts and hands and voices.**

How great our praise
as the world rejoices.
> **We thank thee, now, O God,**
> **with hearts and hands and voices.**

(Mary Scifres; inspired by Catherine Winkworth's "Now Thank We All Our God," translated from Martin Rinkart's German "Nun Danket")

Invitation to the Offering

From the bounty of our lives,
> let us bring forth our gifts
> > for the work of this church;
> let us give generously,
> > as we have been given to generously,
> > > for we are all equal children of the Earth.

Offering Prayer
Let this offering support and strengthen this house.
Let these gifts be put to work in service.
Let our hearts bend toward wholeness.

Sending Forth

Benediction (Isa 55)
You shall go out in joy and be led back in peace.
The mountains and the hills before you
    shall burst into song.
And the trees of the fields
    shall clap their hands.

November 29, 2020

First Sunday of Advent, Year B
Mary Petrina Boyd

Color

Purple

Scripture Readings

Isaiah 64:1-9; Psalm 80:1-7, 17-19; 1 Corinthians 1:3-9; Mark 13:24-37

Theme Ideas

As Advent begins, the scriptures speak to us of waiting. We are waiting for God, for the birth of hope, for the arrival of new life. As we wait, we prepare our hearts to receive the gifts God brings. We ask God to shape us, so that our lives may be ready for the coming of the Son of Man. We watch for the signs that tell us that God is near.

Invitation and Gathering

Centering Words (Mark 13)

Advent is a time of waiting, a time to open our hearts to God's presence, a time to pay attention to God's call. God's love breaks in over and over again. Be awake, for God is near.

Call to Worship (Isa 64)

You alone, O Lord, are God.
> **Come down, O God!**

You have done wonderful things in the past.
> **Come down, O God!**

We need you here with us now.
> **Come down, O God!**

We wait for you.
> **We wait with hope.**

—Or—

Call to Worship (Isa 64, Mark 13)

We are waiting…
in the dark of the year we are waiting.
> **We are waiting…**
> **for the potter to shape our lives.**

We are waiting…
to see clearly what lies hidden in darkness.
> **We are waiting, awake and alert…**
> **ready for God to come.**

In the darkness a candle is lit.
The light comforts our waiting.
> **The light reminds us of the one who is come.**

Opening Prayer (Isa 64)

O God, come to us in our need.
Like a shepherd,
> you care for us.

Like a potter,
> you shape our lives.

Faithful God, we are waiting for you.
Come down to us.

Come down to us as fire,
    and burn away the bonds
        that hold us back.
Light our spirits with your eternal love.
Shape us with your hands,
    that we may be vessels
        fit to receive your presence.
We are waiting, Holy One.
    and place our trust in your love. Amen

Proclamation and Response

Prayer of Confession (Isa 64, Mark 13)
You call us to wait, to watch, to be ready.
But we are so easily distracted,
    busily doing other things.
We grow drowsy and complacent.
Give us wisdom,
    as we prepare for your coming.
Forgive our foolishness and our impatience.
Restore us by your grace.
Look upon us with your favor,
    that we might know your presence.
Shape us into vessels of blessing,
    for we are your children,
        longing to touch your Spirit. Amen.

—*Or*—

Prayer of Confession (Isa 64, Ps 80)
Save us, O God.
Save us from indifference and impatience.
Save us from the distractions of life.

Enter our lives and restore the goodness
>   you have planted within.
By your saving love,
>   draw us into lives of healing and hope.
Heal our brokenness.
Shape our lives with your loving hands,
>   that we might reflect your love.
Come down, O God, and restore us this day. Amen.

Words of Assurance (Isa 64)

God is the potter who shapes our lives.
God is the parent who loves us.
We are the people of God—
>   forgiven, loved, and freed.

Passing the Peace of Christ (1 Cor 1)

God calls you into fellowship with Jesus and with one another. God is faithful and will strengthen you and give you peace. Let us share this peace with our brothers and sisters.

Prayer of Preparation (Mark 13)

We are waiting, O God.
We are waiting to hear your word.
We are waiting to sense your presence.
Open our hearts,
>   that we may be renewed by your grace
>   and transformed by your love. Amen.

Response to the Word (Mark 13)

In these days of Advent, we are waiting.
We are waiting for Jesus, God's love come to us.
May our days of waiting be holy.
May our time of preparation be patient and expectant.

May our Advent season be filled with wisdom.
May we be alert and aware of God's work in our world,
    trusting that the work God has given us has meaning.

Thanksgiving and Communion

Invitation to the Offering (1 Cor 1)

We are not lacking any spiritual gift, for God's abundant
love supplies everything we need. As we wait for God
this Advent season, let us bring the gifts of our lives: our
money, our time, and our skills. God has given abundantly to us. Let us respond faithfully with gifts of joy.

Offering Prayer (Isa 64, 1 Cor 1)

Generous and loving God,
    you give us everything we need.
Surrounded and supported by your love,
    there is nothing we lack.
As we bring our offerings to you,
    may they support your work of peace and justice,
        and bring hope to the world.
As we bring our very selves to you,
    mold and shape us as you will,
        then send us forth to serve. Amen

Sending Forth

Benediction (1 Cor 1, Mark 13)

Stay awake, for God is coming.
Prepare your heart, for God is near.
In the darkness, a candle of hope burns brightly.
In the quiet, God speaks to us.
Go with joy, and remain aware and awake.
Grace and peace to you, from God the creator,
    and from our Lord, Jesus Christ.

December 6, 2020

Second Sunday of Advent
Hans Holznagel

Color

Purple

Scripture Readings

Isaiah 40:1-11; Psalm 85:1-2, 8-13; 2 Peter 3:8-15a;
Mark 1:1-8

Theme Ideas

Firm confidence that better days lie ahead, or at least more just ones, marks each of these readings. "Shall" and "will" abound, along with calls to prepare the way with patience, for the arrival of the new heaven and new earth. Their coming, though not its timing, is sure; ours is to discern and to prepare a path, a highway, and our hearts.

Invitation and Gathering

Centering Words (Isa 40, Ps 85, 2 Pet 3)
Wilderness, exile, tribulation, rejoicing: Your way runs through all of these, O God. May we prepare this way anew.

Call to Worship (Isa 40, Ps 85, 2 Pet 3)
>Lift up your voice. Lift it up, do not fear.
>>**Feeding, gathering, carrying, leading:**
>>**This is how God will come.**
>The old will pass away. A new world will dawn.
>>**Love, faithfulness, righteousness, peace:**
>>**These will mark God's new day.**
>Love needs a path. Peace needs a highway.
>>**Even as we wait, let us make a way for God:**
>>**In our hearts and in our world.**
>Let us worship God.

Opening Prayer (Ps 85, 2 Pet 3)
>God, we are confident you are coming,
>>bringing a world where all will be made right.
>Calm our anxiety, strengthen our patience,
>>and keep our hope aflame,
>>>as we work towards, and wait for,
>>>>your new day. Amen.

Proclamation and Response

Prayer of Confession (2 Pet 3)
>Sometimes, we are not ready
>>for things to be made new.
>Help us, God, to imagine the new earth
>>that you envision for our world.
>Help us see ourselves in it.
>Give us wisdom and courage
>>to hasten the coming of your day. Amen.

Words of Assurance (2 Pet 3, Ps 85)
>God is patient. Think of this as salvation.
>God speaks peace. All will be made well.
>Amen.

Passing the Peace of Christ (Ps 85)

Just as God speaks peace to the people, let us greet one another with words of Christ's peace, as we embody the new world to come.

Response to the Word (Isa 40)

As from a mountain height,
    may we see new horizons.
As in a verdant valley,
    may we be nourished for service.
For a glorious day is coming,
    and all people shall see it together.

Thanksgiving and Communion

Invitation to the Offering (Ps 85:12 NRSV)

"The LORD will give what is good," says the psalmist. Let us share our tithes and offerings, in thanksgiving for what we have already received, and in the sure hope of an abundant world to come.

Offering Prayer (Mark 1, Isa 40, Ps 85)

O God, who restores and makes new,
    let these gifts prepare the way:
        for good news proclaimed,
        for people comforted,
        and for the earth tended.
Through our giving,
    may all partake of an abundant yield of peace.
We believe it will be so. Amen.

Sending Forth

Benediction (2 Pet 3, Ps 85)

Live in such a way that you await and hasten
    the coming day of God—
        the day of love and faithfulness,
        the day of righteousness and peace.
Go now in the confidence that all things are possible.
Amen.

December 13, 2020

Third Sunday of Advent

James Dollins

Color

Purple

Scripture Readings

Isaiah 61:1-4, 8-11; Psalm 126; 1 Thessalonians 5:16-24; John 1:6-8, 19-28 *Sermon*

Theme Ideas

Today, Isaiah, John the Baptizer, Paul, and the psalmist join in a chorus of encouragement and hope. They direct our view to the future, as if to say with child-like excitement: "Christmas is almost here!" Isaiah proclaims that God's Spirit has already begun implementing justice on the earth. John the Baptizer cites other words from Isaiah, calling us to make straight the way for God's coming. The psalmist ecstatically celebrates Israel's return from exile, and Paul calls us to rejoice and be grateful always. If we will listen to this chorus and add our voices to it, our hearts will surely be made ready for the birth of the savior.

Invitation and Gathering

Centering Words (John 1, 1 Thess 5)

What if we live in a constant state of preparation for something great to happen? What if we truly believe God's reign of justice will come?

Call to Worship (John 1, Ps 126)

Come! Rejoice in our God.
Let us give thanks, whatever life brings.
   May those who sow in tears
   reap with shouts of joy.
Let us prepare our hearts and our world
for the Prince of Peace, who is coming.
   May all who weep come home with shouts of joy.
Prepare the way of the Lord,
and make straight the path for God's arrival.
   In prayer, song, and service,
   let us prepare for the birth of love.

Opening Prayer (John 1, Isa 61)

Spirit of God, we give you thanks for drawing near,
   for touching the world in the savior's birth.
Help us draw near to you,
   as we prepare our hearts and our world
      for the justice and peace you bring.
Guide our preparations for Christmas,
   as we share the good news with those who suffer,
      and as we offer our friendship
         to those who are alone.
Move within our hearts,
   as we make a way for your coming,
      by forgiving others as we have been forgiven.

Come, Spirit of God; be born in us anew,
that we may live in your mercy and your grace.
Amen.

Proclamation and Response

Prayer of Confession (John 1, Isa 61)
God of the prophets,
we give thanks for the voices that cry out
and demand our attention.
They call us to put our trust and hope in you.
Forgive us when we close our eyes to your vision,
and when we stop our ears to your promise.
Heal our weakness when we give up on ourselves,
on one another, and on you.
Free us from hopeless living,
that we may joyfully love and serve others
in your holy name.

Words of Assurance (John 1)
Know that we are forgiven in Christ's name.
May Love live in us and through us,
that all may know God's peace.

Response to the Word (John 1:23 NRSV, Isa 61)
Come to the wilderness and meet God face to face.
Listen to the voice of one who cries out:
"Make straight the way of the Lord!"
**God calls us to bring good news to the oppressed
and to bind up the brokenhearted.**
The prophet beckons us to prepare
for the coming of a savior.
**Let us proclaim release to the prisoners
and offer comfort to all who mourn.**

The time is close at hand for the coming of God's reign.
**Let us prepare our hearts with hope,
and our world with justice. Amen.**

Thanksgiving and Communion

Offering Prayer (1 Thess 5)
Generous God, your love renews us
and restores our strength.
With gratitude, we offer you a portion
of what you have given to us.
Receive our gifts, our prayers, and our service,
that your church may become a source of hope
for the world. Amen.

Sending Forth

Benediction (Isa 61, John 1)
The Spirit of the Lord is upon us,
anointing us to bring hope to all people.
Go, and prepare the way for the Lord of Love. Amen.

December 20, 2020

Fourth Sunday of Advent
B. J. Beu
Copyright © B. J. Beu

Color

Purple

Scripture Readings

2 Samuel 7:1-11, 16; Luke 1:47-55; Romans 16:25-27; Luke 1:26-38

Theme Ideas

Glorifying God begins with humility on our part. For Mary to receive the gift and challenge of bearing the Christ child, she first listened to God's message with confusion and doubt. But even in the midst of confusion and doubt, Mary asks, "How can this be" (v. 34)? With faith, she accepted the prophetic promise and answered God's call saying, "Here am I…let it be" (v. 38). As Christmas nears, we are challenged to receive God's gifts with careful thought, with humility, and with faith. We are given a great opportunity as the body of Christ to continue bearing Christ for the world. In doing so, we assist the inbreaking of God's realm and glorify God with our love.

Invitation and Gathering

Centering Words (Luke 1)

O my soul, magnify the Lord. God is worthy to be praised.

Greeting (Luke 1)

Greetings, favored ones.
The Lord is with you.
Greetings, in the name of Christ.
God is with us now.

Psalm of Praise (Luke 1)

Our souls magnify the Lord.
Our spirits rejoice in God our Savior.
The Mighty One has done great things for us.
Holy is God's name.
God's mercy is ever near, from generation to generation.
God's strength scatters the proud,
but lifts the humble of heart.
God's love fills us up, nourishing our hungry souls.
God's grace has called us here,
strengthening our lives of faith.

Call to Worship (Luke 1)

God looks kindly on us when we are at our lowest.
Rejoice in God our Savior.
God has done great things for us in times past.
God will do great things for us in days to come.
Rejoice in God our Savior.
Christ's mercy is upon us,
offering hope in times of despair.
Rejoice in God our Savior.
Christ's love has made us whole.

Rejoice in God our Savior.
The Spirit's power disarms our pride
and prejudice.
Rejoice in God our Savior.
The Spirit's power strengthens our mercy
and compassion.
Rejoice in God our Savior.
Even as we are filled this day,
may we go forth to nourish a world in need.
Rejoice in God our Savior.

Opening Prayer (Luke 1)
Mighty God, pour out your Holy Spirit
on all of us gathered here.
As we follow in Mary's footsteps,
open our hearts,
that we might be filled with your goodness
and your love.
Live in us,
that we might bear the Christ light
for all to see.
Overshadow us with your presence,
that we might truly be blessed
and offer your blessing of love to the world.

Proclamation and Response

Prayer of Yearning (Luke 1)
Savior God, shine upon us with your grace.
We long to align ourselves
with the proud and the mighty.
Guide us to walk with those
who are poor and weak.

When we yearn for riches and glory,
    guide our hearts back to your thirst
        for justice and righteousness.
Remember us with mercy.
We desire to live as the household of faith
    you would have us be.
Help us live according to your gospel
    and trust that all things are possible
        in your love.
In Christ's saving grace, we pray. Amen.

Words of Assurance (Luke 1)

Rejoice! God has looked with favor
    upon the powerless and the lowly.
Christ has come to redeem us from our sin.
The Spirit has strengthened us
    with the power of grace and love.
In the mercy of the triune God,
    we are forgiven.

Thanksgiving and Communion

Invitation to the Offering (Luke 1)

Remembering the great things God has done for us,
    we are now invited to return these symbols
    of our gratitude to God.
Even when we offer small things,
    when they are given
    with the love of Christ in our hearts,
    God can transform our gifts
    into mighty miracles.
Let us fill the hungry with our gifts.
Let us lift up the lowly with our compassion.

Let us remember a world in need.
With mercy and love,
>   let us offer ourselves and our gifts.

Prayer of Thanksgiving (Luke 1)
Just as our souls magnify the Lord,
>   may our offerings glorify God.

Surely, we are blessed.
We rejoice in the mercy that you have shown us
>   from generation to generation.

We remember the powerful promise you bring:
>   hope to the hopeless and strength to the weak.

With joy, we pray in gratitude and praise. Amen.

Sending Forth

Benediction (Rom 16, Luke 1)
May God strengthen you according to the gospel.
May the proclamation of Jesus Christ
>   dwell in your hearts and in your lives.

And may the power of the Holy Spirit
>   be with you now and forevermore. Amen.

December 24, 2020

Christmas Eve

Mary Scifres
Copyright © Mary Scifres

Color

White

Scripture Readings

Isaiah 9:2-7; Psalm 96; Titus 2:11-14; Luke 2:1-20

Theme Ideas

Light and love come down at Christmas, illuminating our path, as we celebrate Christmas and remember the legends, stories, and scriptures that define this sacred season. Light shines down from a star, illuminating the babe who is the light of the world. Love shines this night to show us how to be the light of the world. Love flows through a mother's treasured memories and through a father's willingness to protect a child who is so much more than just his own progeny. Love has defined this child's purpose in our world for thousands of years—a love barely grasped on that night of nights.

Invitation and Gathering

Centering Words (Isa 9, John 1)

Light shines in the darkness, and the darkness flees as the light grows in power and beauty.

Call to Worship (Isa 9, Ps 96, Titus 2, Luke 2)

Christ is here on this night of nights.
Christ is here indeed.
Christ's love has called us here.
Christ's love has bathed us in holy light.
Let's sing with the angels and celebrate with joy.
For Christmas arrives this night.

Opening Prayer (Isa 9, John 1, Titus 2, Luke 2)

Light of the world,
  shine upon us this night.
Shine in our lives,
  that we may shine with your love.
Shine in our world,
  that your light may overcome
    all darkness and fear.
Shine through our worship,
  that our souls may be strengthened
    with the power of your light and love.
In the name of love, we pray. Amen

Proclamation and Response

Prayer of Confession (Titus 2)

Protect us with your light,
  when the darkness threatens.
Redeem us with your grace,
  when sin separates us from your presence.

Pour your love upon us throughout the world,
   that hatred may yield to companionship,
      and apathy may warm to compassion.
In your mighty love, we pray. Amen.

Words of Assurance
   We, who once walked in darkness,
      are now children of light,
      and no darkness can overcome this light.
   We, who once were no people,
      are now God's people of love,
      and nothing can separate us from this love.

Passing the Peace of Christ (Titus 2, John 1)
   In Christ's grace, we become light and love for one another. In this grace, let us share the light of Christ with
   those around us.

Introduction to the Word (Luke 2, John 1)
   May the light of God's wisdom illuminate our hearing,
   that we might recognize the light of truth we most need
   to hear this night.

Response to the Word (Luke 2, Titus 2)
   On this night of light and love,
      may we be filled with light and love.
   In a world in need of light and love,
      may we bring light and love to all.

Thanksgiving and Communion

Invitation to the Offering (Matt 2)
   As sages once brought gold, frankincense, and myrrh,
   we are invited to bring our gifts to the Christ child. Our

gifts need not be shiny or big, for any gift lovingly given becomes a gift of light and love for the world.

Offering Prayer (Isa 9)
>With these gifts, O God,
>>bring light to your people
>>>and love to the earth.
>
>With our lives,
>>shine light into the deepest shadows
>>>and help us to share your love
>>>>where it is needed most.
>
>In your loving name, we pray. Amen.

Sending Forth

Benediction (Isa 9, John 1, John 3)
>Go to be light.
>Go to be love.
>Go to bring Christmas hope to the world.

December 27, 2020

First Sunday after Christmas

B. J. Beu

Copyright © B. J. Beu

Color

White

Scripture Readings

Isaiah 61:10–62:3; Psalm 148; Galatians 4:4-7;
Luke 2:22-40

Theme Ideas

The glory of God's salvation through Christ is juxta-
posed with the ritual presentation of a young Jewish
boy at temple. Even as his family participates in this
common custom, the uncommon breaks in. Simeon proclaims Jesus to be the long-awaited Messiah, the salvation for which Simeon has waited. Anna praises God for
this young child, in whom she sees "the redemption of
Jerusalem" (Luke 2:38). Christmas is a reminder that our
extraordinary God breaks into our ordinary world, our
ordinary lives, and our ordinary traditions.

Invitation and Gathering

Centering Words (Luke 2)

> Even as an old man, Simeon was able to see, in the child
> Jesus, the promise of God's salvation. What do we see?

Call to Worship (Ps 148)

> Praise the Lord from the highest heaven.
> > **The sun and moon,** OIL
> > **and all the stars in sky,**
> > **sing praises to our God.**
> Praise the Lord from the deepest valley.
> > **The mountains and hills,**
> > **and all the trees in the forest,**
> > **worship the Lord on high.**
> Praise the Lord from heart filled with song.
> > **The old and young,**
> > **and all the saints of God,**
> > **sing with songs of joy.**
> Come! Let us worship the ruler of heaven and earth.

Opening Prayer (Luke 2, Gal 4)

> Light of the world,
> > shine in our lives this day.
> As we gather to worship you this day,
> > give us the eyes of Simeon and the faith of Anna,
> > > that we may see the promise of our salvation.
> As we come before you with hope and expectation,
> > give us the spirit of your Son,
> > > that we too may grow in strength
> > > and increase in wisdom.
> In your holy name, we pray. Amen.

Proclamation and Response

Prayer of Yearning (Isa 61, Gal 4, Luke 2)

Father of mercy, Mother of holy love,
  we yearn to turn to you,
    as we seek to grow in your wisdom
      and increase in your grace.
We long to crawl into your loving arms,
  and your never-failing acceptance.
Strengthen the roots of our hope and faith,
  that we may be heirs of your promise
    all the days of our lives.

Words of Assurance (Isa 61, Gal 4)

Sisters and brothers, Christ has clothed us
  in with the garments of salvation.
Christ has covered us with the robes of righteousness
  and the garb of holy love.
As children of the living God,
  adopted into Christ's family of faith,
    let us rejoice in our glorious inheritance.

Passing the Peace of Christ (Gal 4)

Sisters and brothers, as God's children, we share a bond
deeper than the sea. Let us celebrate our inheritance,
and exchange signs of peace with one another, as the
family of God.

Response to the Word (Luke 2)

Ever-faithful God,
  the miracles of Christmas
  bless us throughout our lives.
Bless us with the faith of Simeon and the hope of Anna,
  that we may see signs of your promised salvation
  surrounding us every day.

Thanksgiving and Communion

Invitation to the Offering (Luke 2)

When the time came to dedicate their son to the Lord, Mary and Joseph brought Jesus to the temple in thanksgiving and praise. In honor of that ancient tradition, we come this day to dedicate our lives and these, our humble gifts, to God in thanksgiving and praise.

Offering Prayer (Luke 2)

Gracious God, thank you for the gifts of Christmas
    that bless us throughout the year.
As we offer you our offering in gratitude and praise,
    we dedicate our labor, our industry,
        and our very lives
            to the building of your kingdom.
May our gifts go forth to a world in need,
    as signs of your redemption and your hope.
May we shine with your glory,
    that others may discover your saving love.
In Christ's name, we pray. Amen.

Sending Forth

Benediction (Isa 61, Luke 2)

Go in peace,
    for we have seen the salvation of our God.
    We go with joy,
    for Christ has clothed us with love.
Go in hope, for the Spirit shows us
our glorious inheritance in the Lord.
    We go with God.

Contributors

B. J. Beu is a spiritual director and life coach who pastored churches in the United Church of Christ for over twenty years. B. J. lives in Laguna Beach with his wife, Mary, and their son, Michael, when he is not at California State University Northridge studying film.

Beverly Boke is a Unitarian Universalist pastor in Virginia where she lives with her husband, Nick.

Mary Petrina Boyd is pastor of Langley United Methodist Church on Whidbey Island. She spends alternating summers working as an archaeologist in Jordan.

Shelley Cunningham is a pastor in the Evangelical Lutheran Church of America, and writes for Luther Seminary's alumni magazine, *The Story*, and its online daily devotional, *God Pause*.

Mary Sue Brookshire is a United Church of Christ pastor in San Diego, California, which comes as a surprise to her on many levels.

James Dollins is senior pastor of Anaheim United Methodist Church in Southern California, where he lives with his wife, Serena, and sons, Forrest and Silas. He is a lover of music, intercultural ministries, and God's creation.

Karin Ellis is a United Methodist pastor who lives with her husband and children in Tustin, California. She enjoys writing liturgy for worship and children's stories.

Rebecca J. Kruger Gaudino, a United Church of Christ minister in Portland, Oregon, teaches biblical studies and theology at the University of Portland and also writes for the Church.

Linda Hess lives near the shore in Delaware, where she writes Christian songs and other inspirational works.

Hans Holznagel has worked as a newspaper reporter, chief operating officer of a theater, and on the staff of the national ministries of the United Church of Christ in such areas as communications, mission education, administration and fundraising. He currently serves as development and marketing manager at Cogswell Hall in Cleveland, Ohio, a residence for low-income adults with disabling conditions. He and his wife, Kathy Harlow, live on Cleveland's Near West Side, where they belong to Archwood UCC.

Beryl A. Ingram is an elder in The United Methodist Church.

Karen Clark Ristine is a journalist turned United Methodist minister, an editor, writer, preacher, and fan girl of the Holy Spirit.

Bryan Schneider-Thomas is a pastor in The United Methodist Church, and serves churches as a consultant in art and architecture.

Mary Scifres is a United Methodist pastor, motivational speaker, teacher, and author who brings both inspiration and expertise for twenty-first century leadership in creative worship, church growth, change management, visioning, and strategic planning. Learn more at www.maryscifres.com.

Michelle L. Torigian is a pastor in the United Church of Christ and blogs at www.michelletorigian.com.

NOTE: Several special entries are reprinted from earlier editions of *The Abingdon Worship Annual*. These include: Watch Night/New Year (**Linda Hess**), Ash Wednesday, November 1 (**Bryan Schneider-Thomas**), Good Friday (**Shelley Cunningham**), All Saints' Day (**Beryl A. Ingram**), and Thanksgiving Day (**Beverly Boke**).

Scripture Index

Communion Liturgies Index

Online Edition

**The *Abingdon Worship Annual 2020* online edition
is available by subscription at
www.ministrymatters.com.**

Abingdon Press is pleased to make available an online
edition of *The Abingdon Worship Annual 2020* as part of our
Ministry Matters online community and resources.

Subscribers to our online edition will also have access to
worship planning content from prior years.

Visit www.ministrymatters.com and click on SUBSCRIBE
NOW. From that menu, select "Abingdon Worship Annual"
and follow the prompt to set up your account.

If you have logged into your existing Ministry Matters
account, visit www.ministrymatters.com/awa-subscribe.
Click the "Online Only Subscription" button at the bottom
and follow the prompts.

Please note, your subscription to *The Abingdon Worship
Annual* will be renewed automatically, unless you contact
MinistryMatters.com to request a change.

2020 Lectionary Calendar

Lectionary readings in the *Abingdon Worship Annual 2020* relate to Lectionary Year A (January 5–November 22) and Lectionary Year B (November 29–December 31). Bolded dates below correspond to Sundays and other liturgical events in the calendar year.

2020

JANUARY	FEBRUARY	MARCH
S M T W T F S	S M T W T F S	S M T W T F S
1 2 3 4	1	**1** 2 3 4 5 6 7
5 6 7 8 9 10 11	**2** 3 4 5 6 7 8	**8** 9 10 11 12 13 14
12 13 14 15 16 17 18	**9** 10 11 12 13 14 15	**15** 16 17 18 19 20 21
19 20 21 22 23 24 25	**16** 17 18 19 20 21 22	**22** 23 24 25 26 27 28
26 27 28 29 30 31	**23** 24 25 **26** 27 28 29	**29** 30 31

APRIL	MAY	JUNE
S M T W T F S	S M T W T F S	S M T W T F S
1 2 3 4	1 2	1 2 3 4 5 6
5 6 7 8 **9** **10** 11	**3** 4 5 6 7 8 9	**7** 8 9 10 11 12 13
12 13 14 15 16 17 18	**10** 11 12 13 14 15 16	**14** 15 16 17 18 19 20
19 20 21 22 23 24 25	**17** 18 19 20 21 22 23	**21** 22 23 24 25 26 27
26 27 28 29 30	**24** 25 26 27 28 29 30	**28** 29 30
	31	

JULY	AUGUST	SEPTEMBER
S M T W T F S	S M T W T F S	S M T W T F S
1 2 3 4	1	1 2 3 4 5
5 6 7 8 9 10 11	**2** 3 4 5 6 7 8	**6** 7 8 9 10 11 12
12 13 14 15 16 17 18	**9** 10 11 12 13 14 15	**13** 14 15 16 17 18 19
19 20 21 22 23 24 25	**16** 17 18 19 20 21 22	**20** 21 22 23 24 25 26
26 27 28 29 30 31	**23** 24 25 26 27 28 29	**27** 28 29 30
	30 31	

OCTOBER	NOVEMBER	DECEMBER
S M T W T F S	S M T W T F S	S M T W T F S
1 2 3	**1** 2 3 4 5 6 7	1 2 3 4 5
4 5 6 7 8 9 10	**8** 9 10 11 12 13 14	**6** 7 8 9 10 11 12
11 12 13 14 15 16 17	**15** 16 17 18 19 20 21	**13** 14 15 16 17 18 19
18 19 20 21 22 23 24	**22** 23 24 25 **26** 27 28	**20** 21 22 23 **24** 25 26
25 26 27 28 29 30 31	**29** 30	**27** 28 29 30 **31**